W0010260

"At a time of surging interest in the therapeutic possibilities of mindfulness, this important volume provides clinicians with the vital nuts and bolts details for incorporating these transformative practices into their patient care."

-Zindel Segal, PhD, author of *The Mindful Way through Depression*

"This book is essential reading for any clinician interested in gaining insight into the growing development of the use of mindfulness-based interventions in clinical practice. The authors are to be commended for their clear and pragmatic overview and the thoroughness in which they cover the underlying principles involved in teaching and working with mindfulness in the clinical setting. I highly recommend this book."

-Susan Woods, MSW, LCSW

"Readers will gain considerable knowledge and clinical skills in practicing and teaching mindfulness meditation. Several mindfulness programs designed to help clients with various clinical problems are included. The authors are to be commended for putting together this comprehensive review. I highly recommend it."

-G. Alan Marlatt, co-author of *Mindfulness-Based Relapse Prevention*

"For a book of its length, remarkable in both breadth and depth. An excellent resource for both the novice and the expert in the field."

-Thomas Bien, PhD, author of *Mindful Therapy, Mindfulness and the Therapeutic Relationship,* and *The Buddha's Way of Happiness*

"*Mindfulness in Clinical Practice* is a reader's rare delight, especially for the hard working therapist who wishes to become more skillful from the inside out with the practice and clinical applications of mindfulness meditation in the treatment room. The authors have masterfully reviewed the work of Jon Kabat-Zinn, Zindel Segal, Steven C. Hayes, and others to bring together a fresh and vitalized approach to wed the 2000-year-old wisdom teachings of the East with contemporary methods of psychotherapeutic practice. This book is a real gem and a must have for the tool box for every clinician who desires to both transform his/her own awareness and bring that shift into the treatment room!!!"

-Ronald Alexander, Executive Director of the Open Mind Training Institute, Santa Monica, California; author of *Wise Mind Open Mind, Finding Purpose and Meaning in Times of Crisis, Loss and Change*

"I am so pleased to see this inspiring work my friends Richard, Dennis, and Robert have done in making these mindfulness practices more accessible and useful for therapists, helping others to heal and become more fully functional members of our communities. This ancient inner technology is an exciting new wave bound to enrich the Western sciences of the mind."

-Stephen K. Hayes, founder of To Shin Do; author of *Action Meditation* and *How to Own the World*

"This book is a unique and valuable resource for clinicians. The authors clearly come from rich personal histories of mindfulness and clinical practice, and offer a clear, well-organized overview of mindfulness in Western psychology. This single book provides a practical, straightforward discussion of the roots, research, and clinical applications of mindfulness, in language accessible to a wide audience. The authors discuss specific mindfulness traditions, current treatment programs, and common underlying theories and practices. Clinical and case examples and excerpted dialogue provide clear illustrations of how clinicians might integrate mindfulness practices into both group and individual therapy."

-Sarah Bowen, PhD, author of *Mindfulness-Based Relapse Prevention for Addictive Behaviors: A Clinician's Guide*

"If you want to know how mindfulness skills can be helpful to your clients, *Mindfulness in Clinical Practice* provides a comprehensive answer. This solid, easy-to-read synthesis of mindfulness research creates a broad knowledge base for new and experienced clinicians. The book explains the value of bringing mindfulness skills into the therapy room and clearly outlines how it can help your clients grow and heal."

-Susan Albers, PsyD, author of *Eating Mindfully; Eat, Drink & Be Mindful;* and *Mindful Eating 101*   www.eatingmindfully.com

"This book provides remarkably thorough yet clear and concise coverage of the leading mindfulness-based interventions. Conceptual background, treatment strategies, empirical support, and numerous interesting clinical considerations are all discussed in ways that will be helpful and interesting for all levels of expertise."

-Ruth Baer, PhD, author of *Assessing Mindfulness & Acceptance Processes in Clients* and *Mindfulness-Based Treatment Approaches*

"If you are looking for *the* authoritative book on mindfulness and psychotherapy, here it is. In this intimate, accessible and comprehensive volume, the authors' deep wisdom and practice experience emerge compelling us to consider ways to apply mindfulness so as to relieve our clients' suffering. Regardless of prior exposure to or grounding in mindfulness, the reader will find *Mindfulness in Clinical Practice* immensely useful and informative for its concrete examples, sample exercises, and clear, insightful exploration regarding the interface of mindfulness and cognitive behavioral therapy."

-Andrew Bein, PhD, LCSW, Professor of Social Work, California State University, Sacramento; author of *The Zen of Helping: Spiritual Principles for Mindful and Open-Hearted Practice*

"Mindfulness in Clinical Practice is filled with accessible overviews of research-based programs woven into a beautiful and coherent summary of how various approaches to mindfulness can inform and transform psychotherapeutic interventions. Sears, Tirch and Denton have provided a wonderful and important gift to the clinical community that offers deep wisdom and practical steps to help people move from suffering to well-being. A clear and concise guide, this book is sure to find a welcome home on the shelves of therapists from a wide range of disciplines seeking more effective ways to bring healing into their work and into the world."

-Daniel J. Siegel, MD; author, *The Mindful Therapist: A Clinician's Guide to Mindsight and Neural Integration*; and *Mindsight: The New Science of Personal Transformation*. Director, Mindsight Institute; Co-Director, Mindful Awareness Research Center, UCLA School of Medicine

Mindfulness

in
Clinical Practice

Richard W. Sears, PsyD, MBA, ABPP
Dennis D. Tirch, PhD
Robert B. Denton, PsyD

Professional Resource Press
Sarasota, Florida

Published by
Professional Resource Press
(An imprint of Professional Resource Exchange, Inc.)
Post Office Box 3197 • Sarasota, FL 34230-3197
Printed in the United States of America

Copy editor: Patricia Rockwood
Managing editor: Laurie Girsch
Cover designer: Judith Ritt
Technical assistance: Christopher Girsch

Audio CD – ISBN-10: 1-56887-136-8 / ISBN-13: 978-1-56887-136-3

Library of Congress Cataloging-in-Publication Data

Sears, Richard W., Psy.D.
Mindfulness in clinical practice / Richard W. Sears, Dennis D. Tirch, Robert B. Denton.
p. ; cm.
Includes bibliographical references and indexes.
ISBN-13: 978-1-56887-126-4 (alk. paper)
ISBN-10: 1-56887-126-0 (alk. paper)
1. Mindfulness-based cognitive therapy. 2. Awareness. 3. Consciousness. 4. Psychotherapy. I. Tirch, Dennis D., 1968- II. Denton, Robert B., 1978- III. Title.
[DNLM: 1. Cognitive Therapy--methods. 2. Awareness. 3. Consciousness. 4. Mental Disorders--therapy. 5. Mind-Body Relations, Metaphysical. 6. Patient Acceptance of Health Care--psychology. WM 425.5.C6]
RC489.M55S43 2011
616.89'1425--dc22

2011003641

Dedication

To Stephen K. Hayes, for inspiring us all
to embark upon our quests.

Acknowledgments

As with all things, this book is the product of the convergence of many people and processes. We would like to thank everyone who made this possible, though we know we will not be able to list all of our influences.

First of all, we would like to thank Stephen K. Hayes, who brought all three of us together in a self-development community.

We would like to express our appreciation to our Dharma teachers, friends, and inspirations: Paul Dochong Lynch, James Jiun Foster, Clark Jikai Choffy, Thich Nhat Hanh, Paul Genki Kahn, Robert Fripp, Lillian Firestone, His Holiness the Dalai Lama, Don Myochiriki Siclari, David Kyutoshi Sink, Dean Williams, and the late Alan Watts.

We would also like to acknowledge the support and inspiration of our professional colleagues, friends, and mentors: Bill Lax, Magui O'Neill, Jennifer Scott, Jennifer Ossege, Robert L. Leahy, Joy McGhee, Lewis Mehl-Madrona, Kathy McCloskey, Lisa Fontes, Steven C. Hayes, Paul Gilbert, Sarah Bowen, Kelly Wilson, Kevin Polk, Jon Kabat-Zinn, Elana Rosenbaum, Susan Albers, Randye Semple, Lucia McBee, Andrew Bein, Ron Alexander, Susan Woods, Zindel Segal, Jenny Taitz, and Laura Silberstein.

Many thanks to Larry Ritt, Laurie Girsch, Patricia Rockwood, and Judith Ritt of Professional Resource Press for making this book a reality.

Most importantly, we would like to thank our children and families for their love and support: Ashlyn Sears, Caylee Sears, Carrie Mason-Sears, Jeremy Rogers, Charles and Elfriede Sears, Jaclyn Tirch, John Tirch, Janet Tanis, Ashley Grinonneau-Denton, Jocelyn Denton, Brandon Denton, and Owen Denton.

Foreword by Lama Surya Das

MINDFULNESS NOW or
THE JOY OF MEDITATION

This is an exciting time in the field of consciousness evolution and mental health. Neuroscientific research is starting to catch up to Eastern contemplative understanding about the nature of mind and attention, and the field of mental health is tapping into the therapeutic and awareness-wisdom-developing methods of the timeless meditational traditions. Mindfulness-Based Stress Reduction is widely taught, employed and found useful in many hospitals and other mainstream contexts today. This book is designed to give you an overview of the ever-growing research base and further clinical applications of mindfulness-based clinical interventions.

The literature on mindfulness is growing rapidly as new applications are being found for an increasing number of populations and presenting issues, as well as pointing toward potential future directions for clinical interventions through utilizing ages-old, tried-and-true techniques found in the Zen and Tibetan Vajrayana inner sciences of awakening. I heartily recommend this fine new book as an outstanding contribution to the field, useful for clinicians and practitioners, expert and beginner alike.

Mindfulness is becoming recognized as excellent medicine for our time-starved era. Awareness is curative, awareness is joy, lightness and brightness. Mindfulness is, simply defined, the opposite of mindlessness – and who doesn't understand the problems inherent in mindlessly sleepwalking through life? Mindfulness helps us wake up and fully inhabit and savor the present moment. It is a heightened presence of mind, a nonjudgmental state of total attention to the eternal instant, the holy Now. I don't leave home without it!

Once I asked a Buddhist master what is the true Buddha, the enlightened mind, the essence of all spiritual practice. He said, "Nowness-awareness is the authentic inner Buddha."

Learning to cultivate and practice this moment-to-moment, focused attentiveness in daily life is where the rubber really meets the road on the path of awakened enlightenment.

We're all Buddhas by nature; we only have to recognize who and what we truly are.

With love,
Surya Das

Foreword by Steven C. Hayes

RESEARCH AND APPLY; LIVE AND PRACTICE:
Integrating Mindfulness Methods Into Clinical Practice

Therapists are in a privileged profession. It might not always seem like it, since we deal with so much human misery. But from that base we are able to witness and encourage human growth and courage; human liberation and transformation. In our work we touch the most vulnerable and values-laden aspects of life, even in ourselves. In that sense, therapy is perhaps the most intimate profession.

There was a time when *empirical* clinical methods, however, sometimes had the feeling of techniques for someone else. We applied them, but we did not necessarily take them home. We used them, but we did not necessarily practice them.

In the last decades, something extraordinary has happened. Science itself has opened the door for work on acceptance and mindfulness to enter empirical clinical psychology. These methods carry empirical clinical work into some of the deepest issues of human existence, such as self and spirituality; transcendence and consciousness; wisdom and interconnectedness. These are not methods just to be applied or used. These are methods to be lived and practiced.

That is exciting, but it is also challenging. No one invited therapists to become spiritual leaders, so we cannot enter this territory in exactly the same way as do teachers in the mindfulness traditions. And it would not make sense to import methods that are thousands of years old into a scientific and professional discipline without taking the time to integrate the two. Integration is not easy, however. It requires breadth of knowledge and a good sense of balance. It requires a clear vision that does justice to our profession and scientific discipline, and also to the spiritual and wisdom traditions we are exploring for inspiration.

These authors have all of that.

There are other volumes on mindfulness and clinical work but there is nothing else quite like this book. Not that I have seen. No other volume of which I am aware is as clear, broad, and expressed in such a clear and consistent voice. You can find books on the specific methods of mindfulness; you can find books on Eastern psychology that fail to grapple with the scientific details; you can find edited volumes that are broad but that speak in a tangle of voices. But I do not know of another book on this topic with the scope and consistency of this one.

This book is a comprehensive guide to mindfulness methods in clinical practice written by expert clinicians with a long standing interest in contemplative practice and the mindfulness traditions. The authors know the roots of these methods, both in Eastern thought and in Western science. The range of methods is broad, from Mindfulness-Based Stress Reduction to Acceptance and Commitment Therapy, so the focus is wisely placed on targets of change, not just the formal similarities of these techniques. Given the broad background of the authors, they have the skills and knowledge to explain how these methods can be used in clinical practice, and they do so with an ease and clarity that will reassure those exploring that possibility. At the same time, their scholarly and scientific background allow them to lay out the state of the contemporary scientific evidence in a clear and no nonsense fashion, making insightful suggestions about future research that needs to be done. Finally, they have the knowledge needed to discuss differences in strands of Eastern thought and explain how these might suggest future directions as well.

The consistency of their voice and quality of their writing allows readers to get comfortable with these authors. They are like personal guides you will come to understand and trust, and like a good guide they know what is out there to explore and how best to get into the center of these areas.

When I arrive at a foreign city, I like using guides. It helps me learn the lay of the land so I can dive into specific areas that interest me. If you are considering how to include mindfulness work in your clinical practice, you can trust this book. Let this book take you by the hand and show you the territory and to guide you through that process, for your clients and for yourself.

Steven C. Hayes
University of Nevada

Table of Contents

Introduction

When we speak to therapists about mindfulness, we are often asked, "If I could read just one book about mindfulness, what would you recommend?" Unfortunately, we never had a good answer to this question – the books thus far have been focused on one specific area of mindfulness, or were edited books filled with detailed research. These resources are, of course, quite necessary and important, but this book is designed to give general clinicians an overview of the many facets and applications of mindfulness, in a straightforward and practical way.

But what is mindfulness, and what are its clinical applications?

An ancient Chinese story reminds us to let go of judgments and stay in the present moment (Watts, 2004):

> A farmer in a small village once had a horse run away. Since the village was poor, his neighbors came by and said "What a terrible thing, your horse running away!" The farmer simply replied, "maybe."
>
> The next day, the horse came home, and had brought along a group of wild horses. "Wow, how fortunate!" said the neighbors. "Maybe," replied the farmer.
>
> When the farmer's son was trying to tame one of the wild horses, he was bucked off and broke his leg. "How awful!" the neighbors exclaimed. "Maybe," said the farmer.
>
> Later, an army passed through the village, conscripting all able-bodied young men. The farmer's son was passed over because of his broken leg. "How lucky you are," the neighbors said. You can guess the farmer's response.

Too often, we are making judgments and comparisons, which tend to keep us stuck in the past or lost in thoughts about an unknown future.

Mindfulness is about learning to let go of unnecessary judgments, and about feeling more at home in the present moment.

Much attention has been given recently in the clinical and scientific literature to the concept of mindfulness. At one extreme, a large number of popular books, seminars, and presentations have now added "mindfulness" to their titles.

At the other extreme, the research base on mindfulness-based approaches is booming, but is often too technical for practitioners. Many books and articles leave neophytes confused and bewildered as to how to actually apply these methods clinically.

Part of the confusion comes from using a word that is rather common in the English language. When we give our own presentations, people often tell us "we already do this," whether they call it cognitive-behavioral therapy, hypnosis, gestalt, focusing, and so forth. Although it is true that some of the essential ingredients of mindfulness are based upon sound therapeutic principles that are present in a wide variety of approaches, mindfulness has come to be associated with a specific approach that is achieved through systematic training.

Another problem in the field is that enthusiasm sometimes gets ahead of the empirical research. Although our suffering clients need help immediately, and cannot necessarily wait years for research support, there is nevertheless the danger of seeing mindfulness as some type of panacea. Although we believe that mindfulness can be a useful adjunct to almost any therapy, it is not meant to replace all of the standard, well-grounded psychotherapy theories, techniques, and skills.

In this book, we will endeavor to present that which has been supported empirically, that which is based on clinical experience, and that which is based on sound principles but needs further research.

The story of how all three of the authors came to get involved in mindfulness work speaks to our interest in writing this book. We all practiced mindfulness before becoming psychologists. All three of us were inspired by Stephen K. Hayes, the man who went to Japan in the 1970s and brought the "ninja boom" back to the West. Far more profound than that which was presented in so-called ninja movies or turtle cartoons, the art of ninjutsu held a deep appreciation for the development of the body and the mind. The roots of the tradition were deeply entwined with the ancient meditative disciplines of Asia.

Richard Sears taught martial arts and meditation for years, but felt what he learned about traditional forms of meditation was not enough to deal with the modern problems the students would bring him. He met Dennis Tirch at a meditation seminar in Texas when Dennis was a graduate student. Dennis kindly shared his hotel room with Richard, and they discussed the potential of both approaches. Richard met Robert Denton while they were both graduate students, and the idea for this book was discussed while they spent 2 weeks together in the foothills of the Himalayas in Nepal.

Our unusual mutual interests in psychology, Eastern traditions, and martial arts brought the three of us together. We hope that we will be able together to provide a unique and valuable perspective and contribution to the field.

In Chapter 1, we will provide an overview of mindfulness. This chapter will present the historical background and development of mindfulness, provide a working definition, and explore the underlying mechanisms that make it effective.

In Chapter 2, we will discuss mindfulness for the clinician. Before using and teaching mindfulness to clients, the clinician must thoroughly understand the principles and be able to put them into practice. This chapter explores how a clinician can utilize mindfulness in the therapeutic session and how to develop competency in its use with clients. We will also discuss how mindfulness can be used for provider self-care to prevent stress and burnout.

Mindfulness-Based Stress Reduction (MBSR) was first developed by Jon Kabat-Zinn (1990) for stress, anxiety, and chronic pain. Chapter 3 will cover this pioneering 8-week mindfulness program that incorporates mindfulness and Yoga.

Chapter 4 will cover Mindfulness-Based Cognitive Therapy (MBCT). This approach was developed by Segal, Williams, and Teasdale (2002), building upon the foundations of MBSR. Their pioneering studies showed that MBCT is effective in preventing relapses of depression, and it is currently being applied to a wider range of populations and presenting issues.

Dialectical Behavior Therapy (DBT) was developed by Marsha Linehan (1993a) for use with individuals with Borderline Personality Disorder. In Chapter 5, we explore DBT training, which involves a component where clients are taught mindfulness and radical acceptance to help with emotional regulation. In DBT, brief mindfulness exercises are used at the beginning of every group training session.

Acceptance and Commitment Therapy (ACT) was pioneered by Steven C. Hayes and colleagues (1999). ACT involves learning to accept one's present circumstances and to make a commitment to moving in the direction of one's desired values and goals. We discuss ACT in Chapter 6.

In Chapter 7, we will discuss a number of other group approaches to using mindfulness. Most of these approaches are based upon the work of Jon Kabat-Zinn on Mindfulness-Based Stress Reduction (MBSR; 1990) and that of Segal, Williams, and Teasdale (2002) on Mindfulness-Based Cognitive Therapy. Because these are newer approaches, research is still being conducted and evaluated. These approaches include groups designed for chemical dependency, eating disorders, relationship enhancement, parenting, children and adolescents, geriatric populations, and inpatient populations.

Thus far, the most researched mindfulness programs (with the notable exception of ACT) are conducted in a group format. In Chapter 8, we will explore promising interventions for using mindfulness with individual clients.

In the final chapter, we will identify potential future directions. The literature on mindfulness is growing rapidly as new applications are being found for an increasing number of populations and presenting issues. We also discuss other forms of meditation, such as Zen and *Vajrayana*, which show promise as potential clinical interventions.

We have included an audio CD in this book, in order to give the reader a first-hand experience with mindfulness techniques.

Track 1	Introduction – Richard Sears
Track 2	Body Scan – Richard Sears
Track 3	Sitting Meditation – Richard Sears
Track 4	Three-Minute Breathing Space – Richard Sears
Track 5	Loving-Kindness Meditation – Dennis Tirch
Track 6	Mindfulness for the Clinician – Robert Denton

The techniques themselves are described later in this book. The recordings are only meant to be introductions to these techniques; if we pique your interest, we encourage you to obtain more detailed guided mindfulness exercises from Jon Kabat-Zinn (www.mind-fulnesscds.com), Susan Woods (www.slwoods.com), and others.

HOW TO GET
MORE INVOLVED

This book is designed to give you an overview of the ever-growing research base and clinical applications of mindfulness-based clinical interventions. For those of you who are interested in applying mindfulness in your clinical work, or if you just want to learn more, we invite you to get involved in the professional community.

SOCIETY FOR CLINICAL
MINDFULNESS & MEDITATION

The Society for Clinical Mindfulness & Meditation was founded to bring together clinicians, researchers, and others who are interested in the clinical applications of mindfulness. Full members are listed in a public directory, have access to online forums where they can discuss topics related to mindfulness and meditation with colleagues, and receive a quarterly newsletter listing training events and other news. For more information, visit www.clinical-mindfulness.org.

JOURNAL OF CLINICAL
MINDFULNESS & MEDITATION

Thus far, research related to mindfulness and other forms of meditation has been spread throughout a variety of journals. The *Journal of Clinical Mindfulness & Meditation* seeks to bring the latest scholarly writings together in one publication for researchers and practitioners. For more information, visit www.journal.clinical-mindfulness.org.

CENTER FOR CLINICAL
MINDFULNESS & MEDITATION

The Center for Clinical Mindfulness & Meditation was created by the PsyD Program in Clinical Psychology of Union Institute & University. It serves as a resource for researchers and practitioners to share research and information and to provide training opportunities. The CCMM also provides links to other similar centers around the world. For more information, visit www.myunion.edu/ccmm.

Chapter 1

What is Mindfulness?

Descartes said "I think, therefore I am."
If you don't think, then what?
-Zen Master Seung Sahn

Interest in the use of mindfulness is growing in popularity in the scientific literature, in the clinical community, and in the public (Didonna, 2009a). Although it has been practiced for thousands of years, mindfulness in clinical work is now receiving growing empirical support, particularly in the prevention and treatment of stress, anxiety, and depression. Mindfulness groups for clients dealing with stress and chronic pain were pioneered by Jon Kabat-Zinn, in a program known as Mindfulness-Based Stress Reduction (MBSR; Kabat-Zinn, 1990). Since then, mindfulness has been incorporated into a variety of treatments, such as Mindfulness-Based Cognitive Therapy (MBCT) for prevention of depressive relapse (Segal et al., 2002), Dialectical Behavior Therapy (DBT) for borderline personality disorder (Linehan, 1993a), and Mindfulness-Based Relapse Prevention (MBRP) for addictions (Witkiewitz & Marlatt, 2007). Acceptance and Commitment Therapy (ACT), though made public only relatively recently, has been in development for decades (S. C. Hayes, Strosahl, & Wilson, 1999). Several mindfulness-based programs are now considered evidence-based practices on the Division 12 website of the American Psychological Association (www.PsychologicalTreatments.org).

Mindfulness has been called the "third wave" in cognitive-behavioral therapy (CBT) (Fletcher & S. C. Hayes, 2005; S. C. Hayes, 2004; Segal, Teasdale, & Williams, 2004). Though often linked with CBT, due to its attention to thoughts and behavior, mindfulness can be seen as a core process in all of psychotherapy (Martin, 1997).

Mindfulness is a powerful method, but is not necessarily meant to replace the other techniques of good psychotherapy.

Asking "what is mindfulness?" is a bit like asking "what is psychotherapy?" Although we will attempt to talk about mindfulness as such in this chapter, the following chapters will focus on specific Mindfulness-Based Interventions (MBIs), that is, psychotherapeutic interventions that explicitly utilize mindfulness as a core process.

Though it has been used with a wide variety of meanings, in the context of psychotherapeutic interventions, mindfulness refers to a state of awareness that can be enhanced and sustained through systematic practice. Mindfulness developed out of the meditative traditions of Asia, but the process itself is quite natural, and beyond culture and tradition.

Mindfulness is nothing mysterious. If anything, people tend to dismiss the concept too quickly as being overly simple. Mindfulness is more of an approach or attitude, more of an active ingredient in successful therapy than an artificial, manipulative technique.

You can directly experience a little bit of mindfulness, even right now. As you are reading this, pay attention to your physical body. Most people only notice what they are feeling physically at certain moments, like when they are in pain, or when they are experiencing a particularly pleasurable sensation. Except for those practicing such things as dance, Yoga, or martial arts, most of us tend to ignore the continuous signals our bodies send us. So right now, see if you can sense a particular part of your body, such as the right toe. Do you notice any sensations of pain, any tingling, any warmth, any moisture, any numbness? Is your foot making contact with a sock, shoe, or the floor? Notice if you are making any judgments or thoughts about what you are experiencing, and bring your awareness back to noticing just what is there, as best you can. You can shift this type of attention to any point in your body or do a quick scan of the entire body to see what you notice. Eventually, you can learn to hold an awareness of your entire body at the same time, rather than looking at it piece by piece.

Next, see if you can shift your awareness to any type of feelings or emotions that are present. Are you feeling a little happy, do you feel a sense of stress, any sadness, any sense of boredom, any excitement, or are you not noticing any particular emotion? Many people only notice their feelings when they are particularly strong, not realizing that emotions come and go continuously throughout any given day, any given hour, any given moment. One way of preventing problems is to notice emotions as they rise and fall, rather than pushing down negative feelings until they become overwhelming.

Lastly, even right now in this moment, can you notice your own thoughts? Often we identify ourselves with our thoughts, so this may be more subtle and difficult to observe, but can you detect what thoughts are present in your mind? (If you have the thought that you are not thinking right now, that itself is a thought.) As you gain practice in this, you will begin to notice that you rarely have complete thoughts. Most people do not talk to themselves in complete dialogues. Thoughts come and go in bits and pieces, sometimes in images and impressions. However, all of these thoughts have an impact on your feelings, and even on your physical body, which may show up as a tendency to hold tension in certain areas.

This simple exercise is a basic demonstration of mindfulness. By paying attention moment to moment, we break through the automatic pilot that we so often live in. Although mindfulness is simple, it can also be quite subtle, and not necessarily easy. The concept is not difficult to understand, but it takes practice to be able to sustain this type of attention, and to engage it even in difficult situations.

Now that you have had a brief taste of mindfulness, let's explore more formal definitions.

DEFINITIONS OF MINDFULNESS

Jon Kabat-Zinn, one of the pioneers of the clinical applications of mindfulness, defines it as "the awareness that emerges through paying attention on purpose, in the present moment, and nonjudgmentally to the unfolding of experience moment to moment" (Kabat-Zinn, 2003, p. 145). Because this definition is widely accepted, and summarizes the essential features of mindfulness, we will look at each piece in turn.

"THE AWARENESS THAT EMERGES . . ."

Mindfulness is about "waking up" to our experiences. We often get lost in a mental world of ruminations about a past that cannot be changed or a future that does not yet exist. In mindfulness practice, we practice bringing conscious awareness to our current experiences.

This is a natural process, utilized by everyone on a daily basis. However, just as with physical exercise, regular practice of mindfulness makes it easier to bring awareness to more of our experiences. Anxiety is often sustained by negative reinforcement, through avoidance of feared situations and emotions. Mindfulness encourages a "turning toward" attitude.

"... THROUGH PAYING ATTENTION ..."

Many people equate attention only with concentration, but neuropsychology texts (e.g., Vanderploeg, 2000) teach that there are a number of forms of attention, each with different neurophysiological pathways. Mindfulness aims to exercise all of these various forms.

Posner and Rafal (1986) posit three forms of attention: arousal, vigilance, and selective attention. Arousal is a key component of mindfulness practice. One of the challenges beginners face is the tendency to fall asleep when sitting still. Vigilance refers to sustained attention. Inevitably, when attempting to focus, the mind will wander. In mindfulness practice, the key is to gently and continually bring the mind back, thereby strengthening the relevant brain pathways. Selective attention refers to the ability to tune out distractions. In sustaining your attention to read this book right now, you have to ignore other potential distractions, such as environmental noises, internal bodily states, all the visual input around the letters of this page, and so forth.

Sohlberg and Mateer (1989) describe five forms of attention: focused attention, sustained attention, selective attention, alternating attention, and divided attention. The first three are similar to those described above. Alternating attention involves not only sustaining attention, but also shifting attention. In the body scan, one not only pays attention to particular parts of the body, but also practices shifting attention to other regions. Likewise, when one notices the thoughts one is having, one can practice shifting attention to the process of thinking itself rather than the content of the thoughts.

Divided attention is the one people probably do too often, but there are times we need to do multiple things at once, such as having a conversation while walking. As we know, some people have a lot of difficulty with divided attention.

Training in mindfulness is much like training muscles for weightlifters – one is able to have much more strength and endurance through regular exercise of one's attention.

"... ON PURPOSE ..."

This part of the definition denotes the deliberate, conscious aspect of mindfulness. Cultivating mindfulness helps one to step out of the "automatic pilot" mode in which we live most of our lives, allowing us to discard old, unconscious, maladaptive patterns.

We live in a world that is very complex. There are many variables that we need to constantly pay attention to, going on all around us, at any given moment. Right now, if you were to put down this book and look around you, what might you notice? Within your own body, there are all kinds of things going on. Food is being digested, so you may feel pressure in your intestines or churning in your stomach. You may notice muscular tension in various parts of your body. You may notice temperature variations on the surface of your skin, or the slight movements of air. As you expand your awareness to what is going on around you, you may notice quite a number of things that you had not noticed until just now. Perhaps there was somebody sitting near you whom you were not aware of before. Or perhaps you knew there were other people in the room, but had no idea of what kind of clothing they were wearing. Do you know where all the exits are in the room you are currently in? How is the weather outside? What is the emotional mood of all the people around you (if there are any)?

Evolutionarily, human beings needed to pay lots of attention to the things going on in their environment. However, especially nowadays, there is simply too much going on for us to be aware of it all. We adapted, and we evolved the ability to do things automatically so that it would require less of our conscious attention. Often, we are aware of things without being consciously aware of them. We might call this the "floodlight consciousness," as Alan Watts (2004) described, sort of an expanded awareness of what is going on. It is this form of awareness that allows us to drive several miles while talking to a friend, to somehow dodge all the traffic and potholes in the road, adjust our speed, make minor corrections to the steering as we go along, and so on, all without consciously thinking about it. And yet when there is a problem, such as road construction, we can immediately stop our conversation with our conscious attention, which Alan Watts refers to as "spotlight consciousness." The difficulty, of course, with spotlight consciousness is that it needs to do one thing at a time, and in that sense is akin to serial processing rather than the parallel processing of the floodlight consciousness. When we learn something new we must pay lots of attention using our spotlight consciousness, until it can be ingrained into our floodlight consciousness.

This is a very useful skill to have. However, there are times when our programming becomes unconscious in a way that is not productive, or is harmful to us. Mindfulness works to develop a conscious attention and an attitude of acceptance and nonjudgment to our experiences to break out of maladaptive patterns. Through repetition, this habit, this pattern of acceptance, of paying attention, of being friendly with oneself, one's body, and one's thoughts, sinks down into our way of being in the world.

Initially, when we learn a new skill, it is time-consuming and awkward as our conscious cerebral lobes attempt to process the new information. Eventually, however, through repetition and practice, connections are made deeper inside the brain, affecting our emotional responses to situations within our own thinking, and in the world around us. These emotional patterns affect, in turn, our physical bodies, such as muscular tension, adrenal responses, and other sympathetic system responses.

Although there are times we are happy to coast through life on automatic pilot, sometimes our automatic pilots are set to take us into places we do not wish to go. For example, automatically using worrying and thinking as an attempt to fix problems can keep us stuck in ruminations and worries. Mindfulness helps us to consciously break our automatic patterns of reacting and to accept the moment as it is without making it worse, and therefore to be in a better position to make choices in each successive moment.

". . . IN THE PRESENT MOMENT . . ."

Many times, clients present with excessive thoughts about the past (ruminations) or thoughts about the future (worries). These thoughts are often confused with reality itself. Through mindfulness, clients are taught that they have thoughts, but they are not their thoughts. They have feelings, but they are not their feelings. They are taught to observe thoughts, feelings, and sensations without getting so "caught up" in them.

Of course, in actuality, we can never escape the present moment; the future is only an idea, and the past exists only in memory. Even when we are reminiscing or making plans, we are doing it now.

However, the practice of mindfulness can help us to be more conscious of how we use our present moments. Because many people live in a mental world created by thoughts, mindfulness can help us get grounded in reality.

". . . AND NONJUDGMENTALLY . . ."

This aspect of mindfulness is often particularly challenging. Our minds habitually make comparisons. Although this is not inherently bad, it can cause us to constantly judge our experiences by some arbitrary standard, and we can miss the reality of the present moment. In mindfulness practice, clients are taught to notice judgments as they arise, and not be overly identified with them. Of course, frequently clients laugh at their tendency to judge. Letting go of judgments leads to acceptance.

The concept of mindfulness is intertwined with the concept of acceptance. The only way we can be fully in the present moment is to accept the present moment as it is.

Alan Watts (2004) used to tell a story that illustrates how we don't like to accept where we are starting from. A man was once lost in a small town, and asked the way to another city. The local scratched his head and replied, "Well, sir, I do know the way, but if I were you, I wouldn't start from here!"

Too often, our clients are trying to start from a place besides the one in which they find themselves. They want to be courageous after they've gotten some courage, and want to be happy after they find happiness. They work hard to push away the past, the oftentimes horrible abuses they've suffered. They want to fix all their problems before they look for peace. However, if one cannot accept where one is currently, one cannot progress forward into the future.

In clinical work, there is a delicate balance here. Accepting things as they are does not mean that we like how things are, or that past hurts were okay. We do not want to lack empathy, or negate the seriousness of past trauma. However, pushing away the reality of past hurts only perpetuates them. We need to foster acceptance of past and current traumas in order to be in a better place to move forward. In ACT, the word "engagement" is sometimes used instead of acceptance (S. C. Hayes, 2008).

Because the term acceptance often carries other connotations, such as implying that what happened was okay, Marsha Linehan (1993a,

1993b) and Tara Brach (2003) use the term "radical acceptance." This will be discussed in further detail in Chapter 5.

"Willingness" means fostering an attitude of openness toward experiencing things as they are. It is a concept used in both DBT and ACT, which will be discussed in Chapters 5 and 6.

There is something of a paradox in acceptance and mindfulness-based interventions. Clients are learning mindfulness to change things, but true mindfulness is accepting how things are. Sometimes clients try to use a mindfulness technique to get rid of anxiety, which is a kind of avoidance. However, by allowing themselves to experience their anxiety, it tends to diminish by itself.

"... TO THE UNFOLDING OF EXPERIENCE MOMENT TO MOMENT."

This part of the definition speaks to the active quality of mindfulness. It is not simply passively watching the world go by. Jon Kabat-Zinn (CD included with M. Williams et al., 2007) describes mindfulness as being "portable," not just for formal sitting practice.

In psychotherapy, both therapist and client can actively practice mindfulness throughout the session (Wilson & DuFrene, 2008). If either person spends too much time thinking about what he or she said earlier in the session, or what he or she is going to say, an opportunity for real engagement and connection will be missed.

In formal mindfulness groups, clients are taught mindful Yoga or stretching exercises and a mindful walking exercise to begin bringing mindfulness into daily activities. They are also asked to begin to choose ordinary activities to do mindfully, such as washing the dishes or taking a shower (Segal et al., 2002).

OTHER DEFINITIONS OF MINDFULNESS

The Vietnamese Zen teacher Thich Nhat Hanh refers to mindfulness as "keeping one's consciousness alive to the present reality" (Hanh, 1975, p. 16).

Bishop et al. (2004) wrote an entire scholarly article devoted to an attempt to define mindfulness. They put forth the following:

In summary, we see mindfulness as a process of regulating attention in order to bring a quality of nonelaborative awareness to current experience and a quality of relating to one's experience within an orientation of curiosity, experiential openness, and acceptance. We further see mindfulness as a process of gaining insight into the nature of one's mind and the adoption of a de-centered perspective (Safran & Segal, 1990) on thoughts and feelings so that they can be experienced in terms of their subjectivity (versus their necessary validity) and transient nature (versus their permanence). (p. 233)

Marsha Linehan, pioneer of Dialectical Behavior Therapy (DBT), describes mindfulness skills as vehicles for balancing "emotion mind" with "reasonable mind" to achieve "wise mind." DBT breaks down mindfulness into three "what" skills (observing, describing, and participating) and three "how" skills (taking a nonjudgmental stance, focusing on one thing in the moment, and being effective) (Linehan, 1993b). We will discuss DBT in Chapter 5.

From the Acceptance and Commitment Therapy (ACT) perspective, which is based in Relational Frame Theory (RFT), mindfulness emerges from several important processes. "Mindfulness can thus be defined as the defused, accepting, open contact with the present moment and the private events it contains as a conscious human being experientially distinct from the content being noticed. The psychological importance of mindfulness is that it empowers valuing and committed action, and thus is a key aspect of psychological flexibility" (Fletcher & S. C. Hayes, 2005, p. 322). ACT will be described in Chapter 6.

HISTORY AND DEVELOPMENT OF MINDFULNESS

Although the concept of mindfulness is present in practically all cultures in some form, it was systematized and practiced for thousands of years in the Eastern wisdom traditions.

Siddhartha Gautama, who later became known as the "awakened one," or Buddha, lived in the 6th century B.C.E., in the area now known as southern Nepal and northern India. He lived in relative luxury, and was to one day take over the kingdom from his father. In order to protect his son, his father made sure that the young prince was not exposed to the sufferings of life. However, one day Siddhartha managed to take a trip into the town with one of his servants. He saw people with wrinkled skin, stooped over, who looked as if they had great trouble moving around. His attendant explained to him that this was old age. The attendant further explained that this would eventually happen to everyone. On another occasion Siddhartha saw someone bent over, vomiting, with boils all over the skin. When he asked what this was, the attendant replied that this was sickness, and that sooner or later sickness can affect us all. On yet another occasion, Siddhartha came upon a cremation ground, where there were people lying still, stiff, wrapped in cloth, and pale in complexion. When Siddhartha asked what this was, his attendant replied, "This is death. No matter how much we try to protect ourselves, death awaits everyone in the end." Of course, whether or not Siddhartha literally saw sickness, old age, and death for the first time, or if it simply hit him in a new way, is irrelevant. Many of us know that we are going to die intellectually, but have not yet come to feel it as a concrete truth, an important fact of existence to guide our daily decisions.

Seeing these things, or at least thinking about them deeply for the first time, Siddhartha began to question the point of all the luxuries within his father's palace. On the next occasion, Siddhartha saw a holy wanderer, a mendicant, a seeker of truth. He was intrigued by such a person who, his attendant told him, cuts off attachment to family to seek spiritual happiness. Despite the mendicant's dirty appearance and ragged clothing, he seemed to have a smile on his face. Siddhartha decided that he should become such a person to figure out how to overcome all the sufferings of life. So, even though he was married with a young son, he felt that he needed to go out and find the truth for himself, so that he could make a happier life for his family and for all human beings.

Siddhartha began to study with several famous meditation *gurus*, or teachers, and made rapid progress. However, he began to notice a bit of competition between the teachers. When he had attained six levels of *samadhi*, or absorption (a state of oneness and bliss), feeling connected to the entire universe, totally at peace, another teacher would claim access to even higher levels. Finally, he achieved eight levels and rapidly surpassed even his own teachers. Unfortunately, there was a significant disadvantage to this method. However much Siddhartha, and his teachers for that matter, could attain a state of oneness and bliss, seated in meditation, when they came back out of meditation and faced the real world of daily life, the same sufferings and troubles were still there. The teachers and students basically still had the same human weaknesses, such as pride and competition over spiritual advancement. Siddhartha decided to go off by himself and meditate alone or with other like-minded companions.

After six years of practice, he sat under a tree and became "enlightened" when he clearly saw the evening star. He did not receive a secret intellectual teaching. He found his "awakening" sparked by an everyday object.

One of the great breakthroughs that Siddhartha made, and systematized, was the practice of *vipassana,* "insight meditation," or mindfulness, as a method of paying attention, of analyzing reality.

It is interesting to explore the Chinese character for mindfulness (used also in the Japanese language), as it has been used in the original texts of traditions such as Buddhism and Zen.

The top half of the character above means "now" or "present moment," and the bottom half means "heart" or "mind." In the West, we associate "mind" with our thinking brain, and "heart" with emotions and the organ in our chests. In Asian cultures, there is only one word for mind and heart. Hence, "mindfulness" could also be translated as "heartfulness" (Kabat-Zinn, 2009). Put together, the character can be translated as concern, care, feeling, and sense, in addition to attention, thought, or idea. The character also implies remembrance, recollection, or keeping in mind. This sense of collectedness implies an integrity, in the sense of wholeness, both in ourselves and our relationship to the world around us. It also implies that an important aspect of mindfulness is remembering – that is, remembering to remember to pay attention.

Hence, mindfulness has never been a method of being blank, absent-minded, or cosmically objective. Practitioners who make this mistake are told that this is no better than becoming a "stone Buddha." Mindfulness implies a rich, living presence, full of compassion, noticing and sensing all the interconnections with other people, animals and plants, and our environment.

The *Satipatthana Sutra,* the Treatise on the Four Establishments of Mindfulness, is an ancient text that discusses four subjects to which one can bring mindful attention. The first establishment, or foundation, is mindfulness of form, which includes the physical forms around us and the physicalness of our bodies. The second foundation is that of feelings, or perceptions, such as hot and cold. The third foundation is awareness of one's own thoughts, often related to one's like or dislike of the feelings. The fourth foundation is mindfulness of external objects, which leads to insights about the characteristics of reality.

Jon Kabat-Zinn (1990), originally a practitioner of Zen, systematized and modernized the practice of mindfulness into an 8-week program at the University of Massachusetts Medical Center, which inspired the development of several other mindfulness-based interventions, most notably, Mindfulness-Based Cognitive Therapy (Segal et al., 2002). Marsha Linehan (1993a), also a Zen practitioner, incorporated mindfulness and acceptance interventions into Dialectical Behavior Therapy. Steven C. Hayes and colleagues (S. C. Hayes et al., 1999) spent years systematizing and developing the therapeutic usefulness of mindfulness and other concepts in the development of Acceptance and Commitment Therapy.

NEUROLOGICAL MECHANISMS

This is a particularly interesting point in the history of the scientific study of mindfulness. One of the major reasons for this is that advanced medical imaging methods have been used to study mindfulness and meditation over the past few years.

As a result, we now have a much greater sense of what is happening to the brain when people regularly practice training in mindfulness. Put broadly, researchers have found that mindfulness meditation may result in changes in brain activity, but also may result in longer term *structural* brain changes. Such changes in structure may actually reshape our brains to better handle difficult emotional experiences. Let's take a look at a couple of examples of how neuroscience research has shed light on what might be involved in mindfulness.

Based upon his work in interpersonal neurobiology and his experience with mindfulness training, Daniel Siegel (2007) has developed a theory of mindfulness and the brain, which views mindfulness as a special relationship with the self. According to Dr. Siegel, when practicing mindfulness, we use the regions of the brain that are involved in social relationships to develop a sensitive, responsive, and nonjudgmental relationship with the contents of our own mental activity (e.g., thoughts, feelings, and images). In this way, Dr. Siegel's theory suggests that the quality of focused attention that a caregiver brings to her child while fostering healthy attachment bonds is being brought to ourselves through mindfulness training. Siegel characterizes the quality of attention that we find in mindful awareness as involving "curiosity, openness, acceptance, and love (COAL)." Drawing on the work of many other researchers, Siegel's text, *The Mindful Brain* (2007), outlines the ways in which the brain's central hub of social circuitry is involved in, and activated by, mindfulness practice.

Sara Lazar and her colleagues (2005) have conducted neuroimaging research that reveals an increased thickness in certain brain regions among experienced mindfulness meditators. This thickening was more pronounced in practitioners who had been practicing mindfulness meditation for a longer period of time. The regions that were found to be thicker in this group are known as the "middle prefrontal" region and the "insula." We don't need to worry about remembering exactly what all of the regions of the brain do, for our purposes, but it is interesting to find out what these parts of the brain are involved with, because they seem to grow with increased meditation practice. The middle prefrontal area is often associated with caregiver behavior, and has also been suggested to be involved in the experience of compassion (Wang, 2005). The insula serves as a communication channel between the parts of the brain involved in emotional processing and the middle prefrontal areas. Some researchers have suggested that the insula is also involved in processing information about our bodily sensations, emotions, and the mental representation of others (Critchley, 2005; Siegel, 2007). Dr. Lazar's research is groundbreaking in that it is the first structural evidence of experience-dependent brain changes associated with meditation training.

The field of neuroscience and mindfulness is booming, and it involves some leading figures in the scientific study of emotion. The research points in many directions, and is worth taking the time to explore, if brain study is your cup of tea. It seems that mindfulness practice may involve changes in brain activity that result in healthier emotion regulation, a more stable and nonjudgmental relationship with the self, and even a fundamental shift in our experienced sense of self (Cahn & Polich, 2006; Tirch, 2010). We can only expect that the next few years will bring ever more detailed understanding of how mindful awareness is expressed in the brain.

BEHAVIORAL AND COGNITIVE PROCESSES AND MECHANISMS

One of the mechanisms of mindfulness is thought to be exposure, in consideration of the principles of classical and operant conditioning, operating on the same brain mechanisms that are affected by behavioral interventions for anxiety. Worry can be seen as a cognitive strategy for reducing anxiety (Orsillo et al., 2004). Although thinking helps us to figure out problems in the physical world, it doesn't work so well with thoughts and feelings. While thinking about all the possible things we can do to change a given situation, we are attempting to avoid experiencing the anxiety or other negative emotions in this moment. Because we are "doing something," using thoughts to try to gain some kind of control, the anxiety is slightly decreased, and the ruminations are maintained through negative reinforcement. A vicious circle is set up where the anxiety is not going away, so we think more and more compulsively in our attempts to figure it out.

In mindfulness, we learn to accept whatever is present. Although we may choose to change undesirable circumstances, we must first accept the truth of the present situation. By allowing ourselves to feel whatever physical sensations are present and whatever emotional reactions we are having, and by observing what thoughts are in our minds, we can remove ourselves from the sense of overidentification with them. This process is known as "decentering" (Segal et al., 2004; Segal et al., 2002, p. 38) or "defusing" (S. C. Hayes et al., 1999). This is similar to the shift from content to process that is frequently used in individual and group psychotherapy.

This de-centering process appears to be a crucial mechanism for the success of traditional cognitive-behavioral therapy. In learning to recognize thoughts, and in challenging irrational thoughts, the individual becomes less identified with the thoughts and feelings themselves. By talking to yourself about your thoughts, you eventually realize that thoughts themselves are not so powerful, and they are not who you are. However, in mindfulness training, this process of moving back to view one's own thoughts, feelings, and sensations is explicitly developed. Rather than fighting thoughts with thoughts, one recognizes that thoughts are not necessarily facts (even the ones that say they are) (Segal et al., 2002). Of course thoughts themselves are not inherently good or bad. It is only when we become overwhelmed by them, or when we mistake them for "reality," that they begin to cause difficulties for us.

In the later stages of MBCT, clients are asked to deliberately bring to mind difficult situations, and to sit with them. Inevitably, clients report feeling less anxious about that situation afterwards. This is a good lesson for preventing depressive relapse. Because depression is such a terrible experience, clients typically try to avoid noticing symptoms of depression arising, which creates habitual patterns of avoidance and isolation, which removes emotional and social support, which reinforces the feelings of depression, resulting in a downward spiral.

From an ACT perspective, exposure is really increasing psychological flexibility (S. C. Hayes, 2008). For example, if someone is afraid of snakes, his or her behavioral choices are usually limited to walking away. But exposure allows one to be in presence of snakes and do more things, that is, to feel anxious but still choose whether to sit with the anxiety, observe the snake's movements, talk to a friend, or even pet the snake, as well as to walk away.

HOW MINDFULNESS IS DIFFERENT

Our human brains naturally try to fit new ideas with what we already know. This can be a useful survival mechanism, but can also bias us and prevent us from reaching a true understanding. Of course, this is what mindfulness is all about: recognizing when we are using mental shortcuts, and consciously choosing to let go of them when necessary.

Although there are many similarities between hypnosis, relaxation techniques, and other forms of meditation, there are also significant distinctions. In the sections below, we will explore these in greater detail.

HYPNOSIS

Hypnosis is one of the oldest psychotherapeutic interventions and is still quite popular today (Wester, 1987; Wester & Smith, 1991; Yager, 2008). Hypnosis involves the use of an induction technique in which the client is encouraged to slip into a trance, a deep state of relaxation and openness. Suggestions are made that are directed toward the subconscious mind to influence a person's future perceptions and behaviors.

However, the emphasis with mindfulness is on conscious processes and conscious attention. The emphasis is also on staying present with one's experience in the present moment, not on trying to alter that experience. Although hypnosis has much clinical utility, from the mindfulness perspective, attempting to change one's perspective may become a subtle form of avoidance.

Although a mindfulness CD may sound hypnotic, the focus on mindfulness is on conscious attention. Kabat-Zinn (M. Williams et al., 2007) emphasizes this point on one of his recordings by reminding the listener that the point of the body scan is to "fall awake," rather than to fall asleep. The gentle, easy tone of the voice on the recording is to foster an attitude of openness and acceptance in the listener, not to induce a trance.

RELAXATION AND VISUALIZATION TECHNIQUES

Most clinicians think of relaxation techniques when clients ask about dealing with stress. Such methods as "the relaxation response" (Benson & Klipper, 1975) remain popular.

Ironically, relaxation techniques can often have paradoxical effects. Trying to relax sets up a situation in which a person is trying to make something happen that only occurs when one lets go of effort and tension.

Relaxation techniques can also reinforce anxiety. By trying to escape from stress by visualizing a pleasant scene, the anxiety is negatively reinforced. Even though one may forget about anxiety for a short time, the stressors in one's life are still present. Most relaxation techniques are like taking minivacations. They feel good at the time, and are important to allow you to recharge, but the problems are still waiting for you when you get back.

Mindfulness involves not necessarily escaping from life stressors, but changing our relationship to them. Although mindfulness exercises often lead to relaxed states, this is not the purpose of the practice. If relaxation comes, it is due to our acceptance of things as they are in this moment. Mindfulness is about being present with whatever is occurring.

Progressive muscle relaxation (Jacobson, 1938) involves two steps: deliberately tensing muscle groups, then releasing the muscle tension. The contrast between tension and relaxation is thought to help people feel the differences more acutely, as many people unconsciously carry tension in their bodies but do not recognize it. The client is taught to systematically move through the major muscle groups.

Though one could mindfully pay attention to the tensing and releasing of muscles, mindfulness is not necessarily intentionally aimed at creating relaxation; it is about paying attention to whatever is happening. Mindfulness fosters an awareness of a person's state, and then he or she can choose to use a technique like progressive muscle relaxation if desired. Eventually, however, through becoming more aware of tension throughout the day, clients can prevent the long-term buildup of muscular tension.

OTHER FORMS OF MEDITATION

Technically speaking, formal mindfulness practice is a type of meditation. However, the word meditation is often not used by those practicing mindfulness, because many people have preconceived ideas about what meditation is due to the wide variety of traditional meditative practices. Although various other forms of meditation are frequently used in conjunction with mindfulness, they have different goals and should not be confused with one another. A couple of major types of meditation are introduced below.

Samadhi "Absorption" Meditation

Often, when we are teaching mindfulness groups, people who already have a meditation practice will say they "went off" into their meditative state and lost time. In many meditation centers, when the meditation is completed, people stretch and appear dazed, like they are adjusting again to daily reality. This type of meditation is known in Sanskrit as *samadhi*, or "absorption" meditation, where the sense of self merges into a sense of wholeness with the universe.

Another popular type of absorption meditation is known as Transcendental Meditation (Mahesh Yogi, 1995). This often involves the repetition of sacred words, known as *mantra*, to help arrest the thinking mind and attain a state of oneness.

Although becoming one with the universe sounds merely poetic, or perhaps even delusional, actual brain imaging studies confirm this subjective experience. Newberg, D'Aquili, and Rause (2001) tested experienced meditators and found reduced activity in the Orientation Association Area (located in the posterior superior parietal lobe). This is the part of the brain whose job it is to orient you to your environment, making you feel separate from it to facilitate navigation. When the brains of meditators are scanned, there is less activity in these areas, showing a neural correlate to the sensation of oneness with the universe; the feeling of difference between oneself and one's environment is diminished. Similarly, the Attention Association Area gives us a sense of time (D'Aquili & Newberg, 1999). In meditative states without sensations of space or time, we "lose ourselves," which can be either very frightening or very blissful.

However, as the historical Buddha discovered, when you come back from a blissful absorption meditation, the problems of daily life are still there. In mindfulness, we are training ourselves to be more connected and present in this space and this time.

Zen master Seung Sahn (1997) describes the difference this way:

> Many people like to combine meditation with some psychotherapeutic practices, like the use of samadhi practice. This is because samadhi meditation is a good feeling for those who try it. For some period their problems and suffering all seem to have gone away. "Oh, samadhi! Wonderful!" But this is like opium: you only want more and more and more. And when you practice in this way, everyday mind doesn't feel so interesting anymore – all you want is to continue your wonderful samadhi experience. You are making a special experience that is separate from everyday-life-mind. If you do samadhi, or mu samadhi practice, then you are making Zen somehow "special." You are heading east when you want to go west. Then when do you get enlightenment? But Zen is not so special. From moment to moment what are you doing now? This is true Zen mind. (p. 361)

Compassion and Loving-Kindness Meditations

Compassion and loving-kindness meditations are often included in groups teaching mindfulness (Germer, 2009; Tirch, 2010). Although mindfulness is about being with whatever is present, compassion and loving-kindness meditations work to consciously foster these positive emotions, because so many of us may have to overcome a history of being mistreated, having low self-esteem, and so forth.

Typically, these meditations begin by fostering the feeling of compassion and/or loving-kindness by thinking about a person whom we care about deeply. Traditionally, this might have involved thinking about all the sacrifices and love that were given by our mother in order for us to be here at all, but unfortunately, many clients have experienced a lot of maltreatment from parents. One could bring to mind a kind grandparent, or think of the feelings one has toward one's children. Gradually, this is applied to others, starting with close loved ones, then imagining spreading this feeling toward those toward whom one feels neutral, then toward one's enemies. Eventually, one can imagine spreading this feeling to all sentient beings. One also practices feeling compassion and kindness toward oneself. Typically, one silently repeats phrases like "May I/he/she be free from suffering, be free from fear, experience well-being, and be happy."

A recent study by Van Dam et al. (2011) showed that self-compassion was a better predictor than mindfulness for the severity of symptoms and for quality of life in individuals with mixed anxiety and depression. The researchers concluded that self-compassion is an important predictor of psychological health, and is a key component of mindfulness-based interventions.

A loving-kindness meditation is included on the CD included with this book. These meditations will also be discussed in more depth in Chapters 2, 8, and 9.

Goal-Directed Meditations

The teachings of the *vajrayana,* which is Sanskrit for "path of the diamond thunderbolt," or "indestructible path," are meant to transform all of our experiences into tools for enlightenment. This path, also known as *tantra,* seeks to align thoughts, words, and actions through the use of visualizations, usually aided by sacred drawings known as *mandala,* sacred words (*mantra*), and sacred gestures (*mudra*). The rituals incorporating these "three secrets" can often be hours long, and usually culminate in a state of blissful absorption.

A related form of meditation is known as *kundalini yoga.* Yoga simply means "union," implying the goal of union with the divine.

Kundalini involves breathing techniques and visualizations that activate and align energy centers, called *chakras*, that are believed to reside in key points of the body.

In mindfulness, rather than creating thoughts and images about goals, one simply watches the activity of the mind as it rises and falls. This allows one to make clear choices about how best to act in moment-to-moment present reality.

THE NEED FOR MINDFULNESS

In modern society, the mind rarely gets a break – even when sleeping, our minds are full of busy dreams. When I (RWS) was a teenager, I began keeping a dream journal. Over time, I was able to remember more and more about my dreams, to the point where I did not have time to write them all down in the morning. It left me with a strange feeling – that my mind never got a rest. I was busy all night long.

Some people walk or drive to clear their minds, but unless you consciously use this time, you are likely to be spinning many fantasies, memories, and worries. One of our clients in a mindfulness group staunchly defended her enjoyment of her driving time. However, by practicing mindfulness while she was driving, she began to discover that she spent most of the time ruminating about the past and worrying about the future, which often lowered her mood by the end of the drive.

By practicing being mindful, we can develop a new habit to bring awareness to all of the activities of our daily lives. Mindfulness is not about "zoning out," or escaping from reality, but about engaging our experiences more fully and being more present in everything we do.

Of course, there are times when we need to distract ourselves, tune out, or go on vacation, but if this becomes an automatic habit, life will be missed. Too many people find themselves in middle age asking "Where did my life go?" Alan Watts (2004) talks about the trick that is played on us all. From early childhood, we are always given the impression that the good thing is coming – kindergarten, first grade, middle school, high school, college, good job, quotas to meet, retirement – then we wake up one day and realize we missed the whole thing. Life is a dance. You don't dance with the intention of getting somewhere; you enjoy the dance.

In an era of multitasking and high productivity expectations, mindfulness can help us reconnect with the small pleasures inherent in each moment. When our attention is divided, we are never really present in anything we are doing. The push for multitasking results in always feeling split, or pulled in different directions, or being only 50% present for our lives. Mindfulness can also help us be more present in our relationships – we all know what it's like to interact with people who are not giving us their full attention.

All of our moments in daily life are in some kind of context – parent, child, partner, homeowner, therapist, client, and so on. Mindfulness practice allows us a brief period (eventually infused throughout the day) to be without context, to return to who we really are, as opposed to who we are supposed to be in any moment. We can reconnect with that regularly and carry more of that into all activities and moments. This is known in ACT as self as context, which fosters psychological flexibility.

Mindfulness also fosters a "being" mode, in contrast to our usual "doing" mode. Although this is an artificial distinction, it can be a useful analogy. Particularly for clients with anxiety, it can be challenging to let go of the need to be constantly busy and distracted and to just be with themselves. Many clients also get their sense of self-worth from their accomplishments and are therefore less resilient in the event of failure.

EMPIRICAL SUPPORT

Mindfulness-based interventions are receiving increasing empirical support, which is likely why the professional community is giving it so much attention. Mindfulness-Based Cognitive Therapy, Dialectical Behavior Therapy, and Acceptance and Commitment Therapy are all listed on the APA Division 12 website of evidence-based treatments (www.PsychologicalTreatments.org).

Four researchers from Boston University did a sophisticated meta-analysis of 39 studies of mindfulness-based therapy on anxiety and depression, which covered more than 1,140 participants (Hofmann et al., 2010). Effect sizes were computed using Hedges' g. In the overall sample, effect sizes pretreatment to posttreatment were .63 for anxiety symptoms and .59 for mood symptoms. In patients with anxiety and mood disorders, effect sizes were .97 and .95, respectively, for improving symptoms. The authors concluded that mindfulness-based therapy is a promising intervention for clinical populations with anxiety and mood issues.

Less research has been done to date on using mindfulness approaches with children and adolescents. Burke (2010) performed a review of the research to date and concluded that the current research shows support for the feasibility of mindfulness-based interventions (specifically, the MBSR/MBCT models), but much more empirical work needs to be done to develop a firm research evidence base.

The empirical support for each particular mindfulness-based intervention will be addressed in the respective chapter.

By far, the best way to understand mindfulness is to experience it for yourself. This will be the subject of Chapter 2.

FOR MORE INFORMATION

Didonna, F. (Ed.). (2009). *Clinical Handbook of Mindfulness.* New York: Springer. This volume is filled with information for those who are serious about mindfulness.

Hanh, T. N. (1975). *The Miracle of Mindfulness.* Boston, MA: Beacon Press. A short, delightful book written by a respected Zen monk.

Siegel, D. J. (2007). *The Mindful Brain: Reflection and Attunement in the Cultivation of Well-Being.* New York: W. W. Norton & Company. An easy-to-read, comprehensive text about the neurobiology of mindfulness.

Chapter 2

Mindfulness for the Clinician

When I (RBD) began my graduate training in clinical psychology, I had been studying the practice of meditation for many years, both in the context of martial arts training and through formal training in Soto-style Zen meditation. I felt at that point that my practice was very beneficial for me, both in my personal life and in my work as a beginning-level therapist. At that time, I was interested to see if others shared this experience in the allied healthcare fields. My initial research came up with a sparse number of studies and articles related to the topic, especially as compared to the number that can be found today. However, I was pleased to find that there was some work done to investigate the benefits of meditation on patients experiencing many different ailments and stressors.

Over the course of my graduate work, I felt that although it was exciting that there was such a rapid growth in interest in meditation practice as a benefit for patients, there was a lack of needed emphasis on the practice for clinicians themselves. For my dissertation, I developed a beginning-level course curriculum that focused on theory and techniques in teaching mindfulness-based meditation for the clinician, in the form of a general guideline for a class to be offered during the first year of doctoral-level training.

Authors such as Segal, Williams, and Teasdale (2002) reported that when they attempted to teach the principles of mindfulness without having engaged in the requisite training and practice for themselves, it was not working well for the clients. After they consulted with Dr. Kabat-Zinn, who recommended that they begin their own practice, the interventions were magnified in their effectiveness. This should serve as a cautionary tale for individuals who are interested in beginning to delve into their own clinical use of mindfulness-based treatment approaches. This chapter aims to further illustrate the need, benefits, and challenges in creating a personal practice of mindfulness for the clinician, and provides suggestions for beginning steps in establishing those habits of mindfulness.

RESEARCH ON MINDFULNESS FOR THE CLINICIAN

Meditation practice, and mindfulness-based meditation in particular, has become a topic of increasing interest for healthcare researchers, not only for clinical treatment applications, but also for the potential benefits for health professionals. Many of the most recent studies have utilized current training programs, such as the MBSR program developed by Kabat-Zinn (1990). However, Lesh (1970) initially investigated the benefit of Zen meditation training, a similar practice to mindfulness-based meditation, for master's level counselors. This study suggested that meditation practice led to greater empathy, particularly in those counselors who were initially rated as being low in their capacity for empathy, as measured by affect sensitivity and openness to experience. Schuster (1979) conducted a review of the literature at the time pertaining to the effect of mindfulness on the development of empathy, and concluded that "therapists experienced in mindfulness meditation should be able to inadvertently or deliberately move into direct moment-to-moment contact with their clients" (p. 76). He also reported, "Practice at mindfulness meditation can thus simultaneously enhance a therapist's professional skills and advance his or her evolution as a human being" (p. 76).

Shapiro, Schwartz, and Bonner (1998) studied the positive effects of mindfulness training on medical and premedical students, showing increased levels of measured empathy in those individuals. Epstein (2003a, 2003b) further discusses mindfulness training for physicians, identifying positive benefits and illustrating a method of teaching mindfulness skills. Shapiro et al. (2005) also found positive outcomes for healthcare professionals trained in MBSR, including reduced stress, increased quality of life, and increased self-compassion.

Epstein (2003a, 2003b), Chung (1990), and Twemlow (2001) collectively assert that training in mindfulness can lead to a higher state of awareness of both oneself and others, so that while engaged in interactions, the capacity for the clinician to be empathic is increased. Mindfulness practice can in essence help to "fine-tune" attention in a manner that helps free the clinician from preconceived judgments, and thus strengthens the impact that the therapist has on the working alliance.

THE IMPORTANCE OF
YOUR OWN PRACTICE

The story related by Dr. Segal and colleagues (2002) about lack of effectiveness when they were not actively involved in personal mindfulness practice illustrates the need for understanding and living what you are teaching clients. Our belief is that to be an effective teacher, a clinician needs to understand the important qualities of practice when beginning any mindfulness-based treatment approach. There is a general belief within mindfulness circles that one cannot effectively teach mindfulness unless engaging in a personal practice. This does not seem to be as strongly emphasized in the Acceptance and Commitment Therapy groups, but mindfulness practice is nonetheless characterized as a tool for expanding clinical awareness. For clinicians specifically teaching mindfulness meditation techniques, engaging in individual practice facilitates more effective communication about the processes that are at work when patients or clients are engaging in their practice and are met with common obstacles or breakthrough moments.

In addition to the benefit of increasing knowledge for teaching mindfulness in a clinical setting, the practice of mindfulness can lead clinicians to improvements in their own personal life and professional work. For the clinician to investigate and acquire knowledge of a patient's experience, to attend to and empathically experience the patient's symptoms and/or worldview, and to use this awareness to help create health or behavioral change in an individual's life, is not always an easy task. This level of awareness requires clinicians to be fully present in each interaction they have with an individual. Mindfulness-based practice is one possible way to develop these qualities. Although informal activities to develop these qualities can be quite beneficial, the formal teaching and practice of mindfulness is a highly beneficial way for clinicians to develop their own self-awareness and to enhance awareness of their patients in therapeutic settings (Chung, 1990; Epstein, 2003a, 2003b; Kabat-Zinn, 2003). Collectively, these authors state that the practice of mindfulness can lead to increases in one's ability to be present and attuned to the here and now, an essential quality of a successful therapeutic encounter. According to Kabat-Zinn (1990), mindfulness has many qualities that influence one's attitude, including nonjudging, patience, beginner's mind, trust, nonstriving, acceptance, and the ability to let go. All of these qualities can help clinicians engage in an effective therapeutic relationship with their patients.

In classical Buddhist history, Siddhartha Gautama made a statement that his words were not of great importance when teaching his followers about the attainment of enlightenment. Similarly, in Zen, students are taught that becoming caught in the conceptual aspects of word-based knowledge can cause difficulty in true understanding. The emphasis on words is also not of greatest importance when it comes to mindfulness. Rather, the direct practice of meditation creates the knowledge and awareness needed for understanding.

This is not to say that verbal or written teaching is not of value. If this were true, there would be no reason for writing books, or talking about the practice of meditation to others. However, the words given must reflect the greater knowledge that comes from an individual practice. Healthcare and allied healthcare professionals are quite familiar with the term "practice," often referring to their work as the "practice" of psychology, medicine, social work, nursing, counseling, and so forth. A practice implies continued improvement of skills and knowledge. So it is with the application of meditation practices such as mindfulness.

Segal et al. (2002) emphasize going beyond the delivery of mindfulness techniques, paying attention to the way in which those principles and techniques are delivered to others. In other words, clinicians must have a solid practice and understanding based in their own practice to offer their program in a mindful manner. Clinicians serve as models for clients through mindful thought and intention, mindful speech (which includes mindful listening), and mindful actions.

Through this practice, clinicians may hone their awareness within the therapeutic relationship and their capacity for empathic attunement. This empathy is produced from the capacity for the individual to openly engage in the therapeutic relationship in an open and nonjudgmental manner with awareness and intention. Mindfulness-based methods have the capacity to teach clinicians a unique set of techniques for developing and deepening empathy including, but not limited to, the concepts of awareness of thoughts and feelings, nonjudgment, present-focused attention, and acceptance.

CLINICIAN SELF-CARE

Another aspect of developing habits of mindfulness for the clinician is that of personal self-care. Clinicians are continually engaging in handling the difficult situations of others, and if they are not able to cultivate their own personal awareness, this can lead to emotional fatigue, declines in physical health, and burnout. Healthcare and allied health professionals are governed by guidelines for ethical practice. Within these codes, there are standards of care stating that professionals must offer only techniques or treatment approaches which they are competent to practice. In addition, some standards mandate that clinicians may provide care only when they themselves are not compromised in any fashion that impedes their capacity to provide a high standard of care. For this reason, it is important to become personally competent in the practice and application of mindfulness-based treatments before implementing those principles in clinical work. In addition to this, establishment of a mindfulness practice can aid in developing personal awareness and self-care habits for the clinician that aid in developing resilience to the effects of burnout. Because knowledge gained in mindfulness training does not solely come from didactic preparation, practice is essential. For clinicians to develop a core competency in mindfulness, they not only need theoretical knowledge as a base, but also the completion of personal practice of mindfulness. This helps to solidify the theoretical knowledge into a practical knowledge of the kinds of insights, awareness, and difficulties in physical, psychological, and spiritual areas that may arise when facilitating the development of mindfulness in others. The teaching of mindfulness principles and skills then becomes grounded in a truly competent way.

Beyond this, clinicians can often run the risk of entrapment by their own transferences, misperceptions, and judgments. If our clients are not getting better, we may become overly responsible, with thoughts such as, "What am I doing wrong that this person is not improving?" or we may dismiss the individual in a defensive retreat: "This person must not be following my treatment, because otherwise he would be getting better." In either case, there may be an error in judgment. By keeping an open, nonjudging stance, we can bring an attitude of curiosity, such as "There is something standing in the way of change; let me investigate the current situation and understand it better." Additionally, we may also come to better accept the limits of what we can do to intervene in another individual's life. One example of this is that no matter how advanced the practice of medicine becomes, life expectancy may be increased, but there is an upper limit, and people will die on their own time. An open acceptance of the nature of life can help to guard against the negative effects that seemingly "untimely death" can have on the clinician. This is not to be mistaken with a callous dismissal of life, or an "oh well" attitude. Reinhold Niebuhr's "Serenity Prayer," (ca. 1937-1943) which was adopted by Alcoholics Anonymous, may be an example of this type of awareness, illustrating an open acknowledgement of the limits of what people can control in their lives, and the development of the ability to recognize it when one reaches that limit.

> God, grant me the serenity
> To accept the things I cannot change;
> Courage to change the things I can;
> And wisdom to know the difference.

Individuals working in allied healthcare have often completed many years of education to obtain the credentials and licenses needed to perform their jobs. Professional education, though essential for competently engaging in clinical work, is typically focused on obtaining knowledge and engaging the intellectual practice of critical thinking. This can lead professionals to place a great deal of emphasis on what they know, and in intellectual "fact" or "truth." This emphasis can at times cloud what is directly in front of the clinician, and lead to misunderstanding. Mindfulness teaches us to move beyond a reliance on conceptual thought and intellectual understanding, placing emphasis on the experiential unfolding of the moment. A balance between the conceptual and experiential training helps to create flexibility within the treatment setting, and enhances clinicians' ability to attend to and understand the individuals with whom they are working.

ESTABLISHING A PRACTICE ROUTINE

For anyone beginning a meditation practice, consistency is important, and routines should be established to make mindfulness a daily exercise. As discussed in Chapter 1, common pitfalls can arise, such as misconceptions about the nature and purpose of meditation, for example, confusing mindfulness practice with relaxation. Other difficulties can arise when we place unnecessary demands on ourselves, such as "I have to sit for 45 minutes." Although sitting for 45 minutes can have advantages once a person is able to commit to that time, if we attempt to complete 45 minutes and never quite make the goal, we can become overly frustrated. It would be just as beneficial to complete one or two 20-minute sessions. The preferred method of beginning a practice would be through a formal training program, with an established curriculum such as MBSR, or from a group that trains individuals in more traditional meditation methods such as Vipassana. Unfortunately, such groups are often not readily available. However, many resources are available, such as CD training programs and manualized training books that describe in detail the process of establishing a practice.

We would like to offer some suggestions for practice that can start to develop the process of awakening to the present moment. You will find additional practice elements and suggestions included in chapters specific to different training programs throughout this book. Utilizing those exercises can be a great way to begin to experience and develop habits of mindfulness. As a beginning step, individuals interested in bringing more mindfulness into their daily lives are encouraged to begin by engaging in personal practice. The following outline of activities for a "week of mindfulness" is a suggested first step toward beginning practice. Hint: Each moment is a new chance to begin, and each week can consist of the same (but always different) activities.

A WEEK OF
MINDFULNESS

Day 1   Decide to begin mindful practice (CD track 1)
Body scan (Chapter 3 & CD track 2)
Sitting meditation (CD track 3)
Choose an activity to do mindfully

Day 2   Body scan (Chapter 3 & CD track 2)
Sitting meditation (CD track 3)
Mindful eating for at least one meal
Choose an activity to do mindfully

Day 3   Sitting meditation (CD track 3)
10 minutes of walking meditation (Chapter 3)
Mindful observation (see exercise below)
Begin using 3-minute breathing space
     (Chapter 4 & CD track 4)
Choose an activity to do mindfully

Day 4   Sitting meditation (CD track 3)
Loving-kindness exercise (CD track 5)
Single-pointed meditation (see exercise below)
Continue 3-minute breathing space
     (Chapter 4 & CD track 4)
Choose an activity to do mindfully

Day 5   Sitting meditation (CD track 3)
10 minutes of walking meditation (Chapter 3)
Mindful stretching
Continue 3-minute breathing space
     (Chapter 4 & CD track 4)
Choose an activity to do mindfully

Day 6   Body scan (Chapter 3 & CD track 2)
Mindfulness for the Clinician (CD track 6)
Mindful eating for at least one meal
Continue 3-minute breathing space
     (Chapter 4 & CD track 4)
Choose an activity to do mindfully

Day 7   Individual's choice of mindfulness activities

MINDFUL OBSERVATION

Choose a time (5-10 minutes or more) and a place where you can observe the world around you. Begin your time by engaging in a 3-minute breathing space (Chapter 4 and CD track 4) to purposefully begin to be mindful of the space around you. Begin to observe and report to yourself what is present and to objectively describe what you are aware of in the present moment without placing judgment. Notice objects, people, feelings of touch, sounds, smells, tastes, thoughts, and emotions. The goal is to continuously observe each moment and to describe what occurs without censoring. Undoubtedly, you will find yourself becoming fixated on some experiences, and will find yourself placing judgments, such as like or dislike, on others. Report those experiences as well. You may become aware of analytical thought, attempts to interpret what you see. Notice this, let go, and observe the next moment. You may observe yourself avoiding some moments or thoughts, skipping over the description. When this happens, describe the awareness of skipping or "censoring" and continue describing your observations. After you have completed the allotted time, spend a few moments reflecting on your experience. What did you learn about your tendencies in observation?

MINDFUL EATING

Sit down at a meal or a snack and allow yourself this moment to be mindful of your activity in its entirety. First, allow yourself to be aware of the way your food looks. What are the colors? What are the visual textures and the arrangement of the food? Notice any thoughts or judgments made about the food. Do you experience it as appetizing? Does your mouth salivate? Be aware of how your food smells. Does it smell fragrant, sweet, spicy, pungent, or is it neutral in its smell? As you sit, notice any desire to eat the food. Wait for a few more breaths to prepare to take a bite. Purposefully choose to begin eating, and bring awareness to the motion of your body bringing the food from its container or dish to your mouth. Once you place the food in your mouth, allow it to rest for a moment without biting. Notice the initial flavor as it first touches your tongue. Notice the feeling of the textures of the food, rolling it gently in your mouth. Notice any desire to bite and chew the food, and wait for a moment *longer. Purposefully decide to chew your food with intention and with attention to each time you bite down. Notice any changes in flavor and texture as you process the food in your teeth, being aware that this process releases nutrients your body needs. Resist the urge to swallow the food until it is completely chewed. If you notice yourself focusing on the next bite of food, simply be aware of it and focus back on the current bite. When this bite is sufficiently chewed, swallow purposefully, seeing if you can notice the food as it travels all the way from your mouth to your stomach. Bring your awareness to the remaining portion of your meal, and purposefully choose the next bite. Do this for the remainder of your meal or snack and be deeply aware of the moments and the nourishment it is giving your body.**

SINGLE-POINTED MEDITATION FOR CONCENTRATION AND ATTENTION

Begin this exercise by making a conscious choice to sustain attention on a single object. Find a point of focus, such as a light or candle in a dark room, a picture, or other object. Start the exercise by focusing on your breathing, noticing the sensation of breathing through the rise and fall of your breath, and the gentle flow of air through your nose or mouth. You may choose to use the word "here" when you breathe in, and the word "now" when you breathe out, bringing your awareness to the present moment. When you are centered in your breathing, choose to shift your focus to the object or light. Study the object with intention. What is the shape? What colors are manifesting? Does the object change as you examine it? If you are using a candle, watch the flame flicker; notice the wick in the center of the flame; see if you can discern the variation in colors in the flame. If your attention wanders outside of the intended object, simply acknowledge that your awareness was averted and shift it back to your intended focus without judgment. Continue this single-pointed awareness for your chosen time, and end the exercise by returning to your breathing for a few breath cycles.

Note: For a guided meditation, a facilitator may insert distracters by making loud clapping noises, ringing a bell, or making distracting motions. This allows for the development of sustained attention even in a distracting environment.*

*From "The Clinical Uses of Mindfulness" by R. Denton and R. Sears, in *Innovations in Clinical Practice: A 21st Century Sourcebook* (Vol. 1, p. 144), Copyright © 2009 by Professional Resource Press. Adapted with permission.

We hope that those of you interested in mindfulness-based practice, both personally and professionally, will find value throughout this text, and that the suggested activities provide a helpful beginning toward awakening to mindfulness in your everyday life. With the beginning of a personal practice in place, the remaining chapters focusing on the clinical applications of mindfulness will become more alive, and the richness of the practice will become more apparent. For further instructions and training in mindfulness, individuals are encouraged to access the training programs and resources included in the remaining chapters of this text, or to explore meditation groups in your area.

FOR MORE INFORMATION

Bien, T. (2006). *Mindful Therapy: A Guide for Therapists and Helping Professionals*. Boston: Wisdom Publications. This book is written specifically for therapists, emphasizing mindfulness processes more than specific techniques.

Wilson, K. G., & DuFrene, T. (2008). *Mindfulness for Two: An Acceptance and Commitment Therapy Approach to Mindfulness in Psychotherapy*. Oakland, CA: New Harbinger. This delightful book also candidly discusses mindfulness and the experiences of the clinician. Also includes a DVD with sample sessions.

Chapter 3

Mindfulness-Based
Stress Reduction

When looking through the literature on the application of mindfulness-based practice in physical and mental health treatment, one often comes across the name of Jon Kabat-Zinn. This is no doubt due to the large impact his mindfulness-based programs and research on the subject have made in the ever-growing field of mind-body medicine.

Dr. Kabat-Zinn is a molecular biologist who founded the Stress Reduction Clinic at the University of Massachusetts Medical School in 1979. His beginning program was termed the Stress Reduction and Relaxation Program (SR&RP), which has undergone further development over the years, and is now commonly known as Mindfulness-Based Stress Reduction (MBSR). This program was first described in its entirety by Kabat-Zinn (1990) in the book *Full Catastrophe Living: Using the Wisdom of Your Body and Mind to Face Stress, Pain, and Illness*. The initial intent for developing this program was as a way to help medical patients relieve suffering through the practice of intensive mindfulness meditation techniques, along with mindful Hatha Yoga practice, as a complement to medical treatments. Furthermore, the 8-week program was designed to provide a model for other professionals to apply those same principles and techniques in a reliable manner (Kabat-Zinn, 2003).

The MBSR program is designed to assist patients in the way that they approach their health difficulties, such as acute or chronic stress, anxiety, chronic pain and illness, sleep disturbances, fatigue, high blood pressure, and headaches. Over the past 25 years, MBSR has demonstrated a significant effect on the ability of individuals to respond more effectively to mental and physical difficulties. The program is being used in a variety of settings, including private practices, university counseling centers, hospitals, and complementary and alternative medicine programs.

As discussed in Chapter 1, Kabat-Zinn (2003) defines mindfulness as "the awareness that emerges through paying attention on purpose, in the present moment, and nonjudgmentally to the unfolding of experience moment to moment" (p. 145). Ruth Baer (2003) defines mindfulness in a comprehensive review of the literature as "the nonjudgmental observation of the ongoing stream of internal and external stimuli as they arise" (p. 125). By focusing on the cultivation of nonjudgmental awareness of the individual's moment-to-moment experience, MBSR teaches a very integrated physical and mental approach to working with physiological, emotional, and psychological stress. This is taught through a qualified individual leading the group using guided instruction in mindfulness-based meditation practices, the teaching of gentle Yoga exercises, engaging in group dialogue, and discussions regarding stress and illness. According to Kabat-Zinn (1990), mindfulness has several qualities that influence one's attitude, which are nonjudging, patience, beginner's mind, trust, nonstriving, acceptance, and letting go. This chapter will begin to familiarize you with the concepts contained in the MBSR program and illustrate how those may be used in the context of treatment.

The guiding principle for MBSR is that oftentimes, in the face of discomfort, whether physiological or psychological, individuals will try to escape from their difficulties, and therefore from their own thoughts and feelings. By learning to reconnect with our own internal senses, we can utilize internal guides toward health and well-being. MBSR teaches us to counteract our tendency to fight against our own thoughts and feelings, which too often results in "mindless" action, or action without awareness. The conscious attention fostered by mindfulness practice allows the individual to live more fully in the present moments as they unfold.

APPLICATIONS OF MBSR

The MBSR program has been the subject of many research studies over the past couple of decades. These studies have supported the use of the program for the treatment of a broad range of difficulties including, but not limited to, chronic pain, fibromyalgia, anxiety, sadness and depression, and coping with job-related stress and burnout (Astin, 1997; Baer, 2003; Goldin & Gross, 2010; Grossman et al., 2004; Kabat-Zinn, 2003; Rosenzweig et al., 2007; Lush et al., 2009; Shapiro et al., 2003; Vieten & Astin, 2008; Weissbecker et al., 2002) We will provide a brief description of some of the results of these studies, including some of the most recent findings, in an effort to exemplify the positive benefits of this pioneering program.

The reduction of stress, anxiety, and mood difficulties through MBSR training has been documented by a number of authors (Baer, 2003, 2006; Farb et al., 2010; Goldin & Gross, 2010; Kabat-Zinn, 1990, 2003; Kabat-Zinn et al., 1992; J. J. Miller, Fletcher, & Kabat-Zinn, 1995). These studies demonstrated effectiveness in reducing overall levels of anxiety and maintaining those benefits over time, showing positive benefits even at a 3-year followup. Biegel et al. (2009) found significant decreases in anxiety and depression, reduced reports of somatic distress, improved quality of sleep, and increased self-esteem among adolescent MBSR participants. Farb et al. (2010) studied neural imaging data for individuals who were trained in MBSR, and found that there were shifts in neural expressions of sadness and depression. This data suggests potential neurological mechanisms of action of mindfulness training, and for the resulting benefits in mood.

MBSR has also shown promising results for difficulties associated with chronic illness, such as cancer and diabetes. Lengacher et al. (2009) and Kievet-Stijnen et al. (2008) both examined the effects that MBSR training had on cancer survivors and their feelings of psychological well-being. Their results suggest that MBSR is a beneficial addition to cancer treatment, due to the participants' significant reduction in the fear of cancer recurrence, reductions in state and trait anxiety, and reports of decreased feelings of depression. This study also showed significant improvements in the participants' ratings of physical functioning with regard to health limitations. In addition, Kievet-Stijnen et al. (2008) showed increases in reported quality of life, feelings of joy, and energy. They also demonstrated decreases in feelings of tension and physiological symptoms. These positive benefits appear to be sustained over time, as reported in a 1-year followup. Participants of the MBSR group also reported decreases in disturbance of mood, such as depression and anger.

Shapiro et al. (2003) also investigated the addition of MBSR training in breast cancer treatment and the effects that it had on sleep disturbances. They concluded that MBSR is a promising intervention in helping to improve the quality of sleep in women with breast cancer, because of the reduction in levels of stress related to cancer treatment.

Rosenzweig et al. (2007) investigated the effects of MBSR with individuals diagnosed with type-II diabetes. Their results showed improvements in glycemic regulation that could not be accounted for by changes in lifestyle, such as diet, medication, or exercise. They proposed that the learned ability to reduce reactivity to stress helps to interrupt the physiological stress responses that lead to difficulties in glycemic regulation.

In Kabat-Zinn's original work at the University of Massachusetts, the MBSR program demonstrated benefits for individuals suffering from chronic pain disorders. Kabat-Zinn et al. (1985, 1986) demonstrated an increased ability of patients to respond to their experience of pain and improved self-regulation of pain responses. Furthermore, there appeared to be continued benefits for individuals who maintained practice of skills 4 years following participation. More recently, Rosenzweig et al. (2010) conducted a longitudinal study investigating the effects of an MBSR program on patients' experience of pain, beliefs about quality of life, and their incidence of psychological symptoms. This study showed significant improvements consistent with previous findings. In particular, patients who were experiencing back or neck pain, and two or more co-morbid pain conditions, found the most benefit from MBSR. Although still showing benefits, individuals diagnosed with fibromyalgia demonstrated less significant change. Weissbecker et al. (2002) and Sephton et al. (2007) also investigated the effects of MBSR for women diagnosed with fibromyalgia. Their focus was on the experience of a sense of coherence, or the feeling that "life makes sense," and the alleviation of depressive symptoms. Based on those studies, although the level of pain was not investigated, the women showed positive changes in their feelings about life, and in the reduction of both cognitive and somatic symptoms of depression. This suggests that MBSR can be an effective adjunctive treatment for individuals with fibromyalgia.

PRINCIPLES OF MBSR

In an effort to give a distilled introduction to the MBSR program, and what drives its efficacy, we will discuss the guiding principles and techniques used in the program. It is important to note that MBSR is not generally viewed as a psychotherapy or medical therapy, but is an educational program aimed to teach group participants to alter habits of attention and observation to develop a greater awareness of themselves and each moment of experience. Of course, there are theoretical underpinnings to the teaching and practice of mindfulness, as discussed in Chapter 1.

Kabat-Zinn (1990) identifies nonjudgment as a key ingredient for developing mindful awareness. According to him, nonjudgment refers to the ability to experience something in one's life without making an attribution of "good," "bad," or "neutral." Judging leads to automatic reactions because of the attribution made, and tends to lock us into an unconscious response. In contrast to this, nonjudgment fosters greater levels of mindfulness because of the investigative need to understand. Through practice, individuals can learn to attend to each aspect of their experience or situation without immediately making judgments about it. Given that the process of making judgments is often done without conscious awareness, the activities of mindful practice attempt to reinstate the conscious process of observation. In order to do this, one must keep a continued state of investigative curiosity and openness to experience. Kabat-Zinn identifies with the concept of beginner's mind, and utilizes this idea throughout his MBSR program.

"Beginner's mind" is a reference from the writings of the Zen teacher Shunryu Suzuki (2006), who stated that, "In the beginner's mind there are many possibilities, but in the expert's there are few" (p. 21). Suzuki posits that when one loses this beginner's mind, one begins to believe that one has learned all there is to learn regarding that topic. If, then, there is a loss of beginner's mind toward one's own experience, there are no longer any new possibilities. In essence, when individuals obtain a sense of having gained some kind of knowledge that they believe is "fact," this can often present a block to new learning or experience. For example, if there was a belief that the world was flat, and that if one sailed too far from land he or she would fall off the edge, this would prove to be a deterrent for exploration. The same happens in our daily life experience. If we engage in activities with an expectation of what that experience will be, we are more likely to be disconnected from our experiences. We may judge ourselves based on what we believe to be true, rather than to embody true self-compassion and acceptance.

Mindfulness aims to correct this block by developing our capacity to view each new moment with fresh eyes. We learn that each time we do something, it is new, even if we have done a similar activity in the past. In order to do this, we must learn to trust. Trust in this sense is not the trust in what others tell us, but rather a trust in our own innate capacity for developing awareness and in our ability to see our potential and our limits. Kabat-Zinn (1994) explains trust as being an ability to look internally and have faith in the process by which one can observe, be open, and be reflective of one's own observations in a manner that leads to a deeper understanding. Too often, individuals allow commentary from outside of themselves to lead to an invalidation of what they experience. Mindfulness teaches that you have the authority to continually become yourself in each moment. When this trust develops, it allows you to be open not only to your own experience, but to also investigate differing perspectives with more clarity and less defensiveness.

MBSR PRACTICES

The MBSR program consists of many practices that help individuals cultivate awareness. These techniques are taught and built upon in a progressive manner throughout the 8-week program. Participants practice together in the group and are given homework to practice daily to help foster new habits. The next few paragraphs will introduce some of the main techniques and briefly discuss the rationale for their inclusion in the program.

THE BODY SCAN

The body scan is typically one of the first techniques employed in the MBSR program because it provides a foundational basis on which to build other aspects of awareness. The body scan is traditionally practiced while participants are lying down, and typically lasts for approximately 45 minutes. To an outside observer, the group may appear to be resting, or "doing nothing." However, while the body scan is a practice of physical "non-doing," participants focus their awareness on individual parts of their body, creating a "scan" from toe to head for areas of tension and discomfort, as well as areas that are free from tension and discomfort. Individuals who struggle with chronic difficulties, such as pain, often become focused on the experience of pain and miss the awareness that likely a greater number of areas are pain free! Repetition of the body scan throughout the program helps participants to have a more complete view of their own physical state and prepare them for other mindfulness meditation practices. Additionally, although the intention in the body scan is to develop awareness, the result can often be relaxation of the body and reduction of feelings of stress and pain. Though deep relaxation can occur during the body scan, the aim is not to fall asleep, but rather to "fall awake" (Kabat-Zinn, 1990). This is referring to the active arousal of awareness of each region of one's body, in contrast with the shifts in brain activity seen during the initiation of sleep. If participants have difficulty engaging in the body scan without falling asleep, they are encouraged to attempt the scan with their eyes open to help maintain wakefulness. We have included a script version of a body scan as an example of how a group leader may lead a body scan inspired by this author's (RBD) experience with Thich Nhat Hanh, and on his exercise called "Deep Relaxation" (Hanh, 2001). Other versions may be found in many resources, including Kabat-Zinn's (1990) original text on MBSR.

BODY SCAN

Lie or sit down in a comfortable position. Allow your arms and legs to relax.

As you breathe in, become aware of your whole body lying or sitting, and become aware of the relaxation of being still. Feel the areas of your body that come into contact with the floor or the chair; your toes, heels, the back of your legs, your back, your arms, your neck, and the back of your head. With the completion of each breath, let your body relax deeper into the floor or chair. Let go of your worries, your tension, and any negativity that you may be holding on to.

As you breathe in, feel your abdomen rising, and as you breathe out, feel it fall again. Take a moment to feel that rise and fall.

As you breathe in, become aware of your feet. Allow your feet to feel relaxed, and as you breathe out smile to those two feet. Thank your feet for all that they do for you, be thankful that you have feet; to walk, run, drive your car, and to do any other activities that require feet.

As you breathe in, become aware of your legs. Allow your legs to relax, smile to your legs, and allow your legs to become relaxed. Feel the appreciation you have for your legs; for letting you do the things you do that require legs. Allow them to sink into the floor or chair and let any remaining tension release.

Breathing in, become aware of your two hands. As you breathe in, release any tension that you may be holding in your hands. Appreciate how wonderful it is to have hands and send your hands positive feelings. Thank them for allowing you to do all the activities you do that require hands.

Continue this type of activity for your arms, back, heart, stomach, eyes, ears, and other parts of the body using the same pattern as above.

If there is any particular part of your body that gives you pain, or has to work extra hard, be aware of that part of your body and send it your love, and thank it for trying so hard. Be aware that there are other parts of your body that are still strong and allow these parts of your body to send some of their strength to assist that ailing part.

Finally, be aware of your body as a whole, relaxed against the chair or floor, and just enjoy that relaxation.

To end, stretch slowly and allow your eyes to open. Allow that sense of open awareness to continue with you throughout the day.

SITTING MEDITATION

Formal sitting meditation is an integral part of the MBSR program, which is no surprise given that the roots of the program are grounded in traditional Buddhist meditation. Although meditation practice is more than just a "technique," there is a basic format for developing and cultivating mindful awareness through sitting meditation. The "technique" of sitting meditation is simply to allow feelings, thoughts, and sensations to be observed without placing value judgments on them. Rather than categorize our experiences through the evaluation of "good" and "bad" thoughts, feelings, or sensations (as mentioned in the discussion of beginner's mind), one cultivates the simple awareness of these experiences. This awareness may not be experienced as pleasant, but it teaches the individual to live in the present and with an attitude of acceptance.

There are many forms of meditation, some of which can have specific goals for states of consciousness or other outcomes. These types of meditation are very valid practices, but differ slightly from the concepts of mindful awareness. This can often be a difficult switch for individuals who have had experience with other types of meditation. Mindfulness-based meditation, rather than working with a specific object for meditation, focuses on simply perceiving whatever one is feeling, thinking, perceiving, or doing in the current moment. Therefore, in essence, the object of focus changes as each experience unfolds, with the individual letting go of each occurrence as soon as it ends. Participants of MBSR programs are advised to practice sitting meditation for 45 minutes every day. To the novice, 45 minutes can be a daunting task, and should not be viewed rigidly. Participants should set a realistic goal that they can reach. A single 45-minute session can be very beneficial, but if each time they set a goal for 45 minutes and can only make it to 30 minutes, they may begin to feel as if they "can't meditate properly," even though 30 minutes is a great meditation time! Engaging in two 20-minute sessions a day may allow individuals to more effectively meet their goals for practice.

HATHA YOGA

MBSR also adds Hatha Yoga exercises as part of the training. Although this practice is not formally a practice of mindfulness-based meditation, individuals are taught to use mindful acceptance throughout the stretching exercises. MBSR was developed with and taught to individuals who have multiple difficulties, including chronic pain, and the Yoga exercises are not done with the intent of developing better physical fitness (even if this can be an added benefit in the long run). Yoga can be another form of meditation, a formal practice of mindful movement, and provides the opportunity to explore the limits of the range of motion. Yoga teaches the individual to accept these limits and relax into the poses, rather than to meet limits by pushing through with force. This can be particularly important for individuals with chronic pain and/or physical disabilities that limit their range of motion. A typical response can be to tighten the muscles around an area in which pain is experienced in an attempt to push through. Physiologically, this can cause additional tightening around the focus of the pain and ultimately an increase in that pain sensation. By accepting the limit and using the awareness of our bodies, one can let go of the tendency to push through, thereby relaxing the muscle tension around the focus point. These same principles are later applied to emotions and thoughts.

One difficulty that can arise is that a background thought of "I am doing Yoga to relax my muscles and get less pain" tends to interfere with the practice. The purpose of Yoga is simply being aware and accepting experience without unnecessary judgment. If a reduction of pain happens to occur, the participant can be aware of that change. By working with the body and remaining aware of breathing, participants can be more mindful of their own bodies and the signals that are given in daily life, which act as a beacon for avoiding engaging in harmful behaviors. Another beneficial side effect of Yoga is that gentle stretching exercises prior to formal sitting meditation make the individual feel more comfortable and able to sit for longer periods (which is what Yoga was historically designed for).

DAILY ACTIVITIES

Although sitting meditation is central to the practice of mindfulness, participants of the MBSR program are taught and encouraged to extend their practice to daily activities such as eating, walking, cleaning, driving, and so on. The intention behind this extension is that mindfulness is meant to bring awareness throughout the activities of life. If the practice is carved out for only certain times during the day, does this mean that the remaining parts of the day are mindless? By extending practice to daily life, individuals become active participants in life, rather than having a view that they are passive receivers of life's impact or that life happens to them (Kabat-Zinn, 1990, p. 138). Individuals enter the driver's seat, becoming more accepting of conditional situations, and more responsible for their responses to stress, pain, and illness. One way to begin this extension into daily life is through the practice of walking meditation.

MINDFUL WALKING

Mindful walking is a formal practice of meditation that brings individuals' awareness to the connectivity of their body's movement and to the ground that they walk over. Rather than focusing on the destination of the walking, individuals are instructed on how to be aware of the process of walking. If you observe a toddler beginning to walk, you will notice how intently that child needs to focus on balance and movement. As walking becomes proficient, the "expert mind" begins, and walking can become an automatic process that needs little awareness in one's conscious mind. By reclaiming conscious awareness through walking meditation, the experience can become very alive. To do this, in the MBSR program, the participants walk slowly on a straight line, purposefully walking for the sake of walking, rather than to meet a destination. More informal practices of walking meditation can then be carried on outside of the group in the midst of daily activities. Each destination reached as one moves throughout the day is a "step" in the direction of cultivating continual mindful awareness.

We have included a brief example of a script that can be used in introducing and practicing walking meditation (Denton & Sears, 2009), and a brief description of the entire 8-week MBSR program (Kabat-Zinn, 1990).

INSTRUCTIONS ON WALKING MEDITATION

Start by standing in a neutral body posture and focus your awareness on your breath. Allow your breath to rise and fall naturally. When you are aware of your breathing, begin to walk, taking only one step with each inhalation and exhalation. Allow your steps to be determined by your breath. If you have a longer breath, do not shorten it, but rather wait for the next step. As you are doing this exercise, you may silently repeat a series of statements to yourself. One example is as follows:

> *Breathing in, I take a step.*
> *Breathing out, I take a step.*
> *With each step I feel refreshed.*
> *I am aware of myself in the moment.*

Do this walking exercise for approximately 10 to 20 minutes.

OUTLINE OF 8-WEEK
MBSR GROUP

Each class consists of leading meditations, Hatha Yoga movement exercises, mindfulness education, and group discussion.

Session 1: Introduction to the program and program philosophy; Eating a raisin; Teaching the foundations of mindfulness practice; Discovering that there is "More right with you than wrong"; Introduction to body scan meditation.

Session 2: Learning patience; Working with the perceptions of the mind; Learning to respond to the distracted mind; Beginning to track pleasant events; Begin bringing awareness to daily mindful activities (e.g., brushing teeth, driving car).

Session 3: Developing the attitude of "Non-Striving"; Introduction to awareness of the breath.

Session 4: Development of the attitude of Nonjudging; Learning about responding vs. reacting; Formal sitting meditation practice; Beginning basic movement meditation through Hatha Yoga.

Session 5: Sitting meditation (beginning to increase the time sitting); Discussion about mindfulness in daily life and personalizing practice.

Session 6: Development of acceptance and letting go; Learning skillful communication; Walking meditation.

Session 7: Sitting meditation; Mindful movement; Learning how to continue mindful practice on your own.

Session 8: Sitting meditation; Mindful movement; Making a commitment to continue to practice; Course review and group reflection.

TRAINING IN MBSR

For individuals interested in either learning to lead MBSR groups or in participating in an MBSR program, there are now many options for doing so. Although the MBSR program was originally only offered through the University of Massachusetts' Stress Reduction Clinic, increases in opportunities have flourished with the success of the program and the development of many qualified professionals offering training in MBSR. As discussed in Chapter 2, we believe that competent professionals offering any mindfulness-based program should be active participants in their own mindful practice. MBSR is no exception to this, which is evident to any individual who attends training workshops to offer MBSR in their clinic or practice.

FOR MORE INFORMATION

Kabat-Zinn, J. (1990). *Full Catastrophe Living: Using the Wisdom of Your Body and Mind to Face Stress, Pain, and Illness.* New York: Dell. This book is a must read for anyone interested in MBSR. It outlines the MBSR program, talks about the underpinnings of the program, and explains the nature of stress.

http://www.umassmed.edu/cfm – This is the website of the University of Massachusetts Medical School Center for Mindfulness in Medicine, Health Care, and Society, founded by Jon Kabat-Zinn. It contains information about MBSR, training programs, and mindfulness practice recordings.

Chapter 4

Mindfulness-Based Cognitive Therapy

Among the "3rd Generation" cognitive and behavioral therapies, Mindfulness-Based Cognitive Therapy (MBCT) is a powerful example of how meticulously psychologists can blend Eastern philosophy and a Western emphasis on evidence-based treatments. MBCT was designed to help better prevent depressive relapse, through a cost-effective and time-limited group therapy format (Segal et al., 2002). Over the course of the last 10 years, outcome research has established that MBCT can significantly reduce the rates of relapse for persons who have had three or more depressive episodes (Ma & Teasdale, 2004; Teasdale et al., 2000). Additionally, fMRI research involving MBCT training has revealed distinct patterns of brain activity that emerge after mindfulness training through MBCT (Farb et al., 2007). These patterns seem to involve the development of a different, more present-focused sense of self. As we have seen, mindfulness interventions in general have been demonstrated to have significant clinical effectiveness across a variety of applications (Hofmann et al., 2010). At present, the body of evidence for MBCT and other mindfulness-based therapies is rapidly growing, and it is reasonable to predict that new research will clarify and further establish the utility of MBCT in the coming years.

Although MBCT has its roots in Buddhist meditation as distilled through Jon Kabat-Zinn's Mindfulness-Based Stress Reduction (MBSR) (Kabat-Zinn, 1990), MBCT is also clearly based upon Cognitive Therapy (CT; Beck et al., 1979). In order to understand MBCT, its rationale, and how it came into being in the first place, we need to spend some time becoming familiar with CT itself.

At the time of MBCT's design, Beckian CT had established a dominant cognitive behavioral therapy (CBT) theory in its "Cognitive Model of Depression" (Beck et al., 1979). The Cognitive Model claims that thoughts, assumptions, and core beliefs hold a strong determining influence over human emotions and behavior. Such beliefs are also said to play a causal role in emotional disorders, according to CT theory.

Therapies based upon this model have been validated in hundreds of outcome studies and randomized controlled trials. This body of outcome research establishes a relatively high degree of clinical efficacy for CT across at least 16 different psychiatric disorders (Butler et al., 2006).

Despite this range of application, Beckian CT was originally developed as a treatment for depression, and the Cognitive Model is, in essence, a model of depressive cognition. Beyond this, CT for depression is focused primarily on the relationships among thoughts, emotions, and behaviors during a *current* depressive episode (Beck et al., 1979). Although there are some techniques within the cognitive therapy literature that relate to relapse prevention, the Cognitive Model of depression is a model of a depressive episode in progress, and depression's origins in a person's early life. Accordingly, the model looks at historical influences interacting with current stressors to result in depressive symptoms. The model did not address an individual's vulnerability to future depressive episodes. MBCT aims to expand the model, and to more fully address vulnerability to depressive relapse and recurrence (Segal et al., 2002).

Interestingly, the story of how MBCT was imagined and developed has become widely known, as it is warmly and openly discussed in the original MBCT text, *Mindfulness-Based Cognitive Therapy for Depression: A New Approach To Preventing Relapse* (Segal, Williams, & Teasdale, 2002) (known colloquially as "The Green Book"). The inclusion of this compelling narrative, written throughout a scholarly text on a form of cognitive psychotherapy, is a clear indication of the distinctively authentic tone and humanistic character that has come to characterize this movement in CBT. We will briefly recap this story, as it helps to explain the roots and aims of MBCT.

Zindel Segal, Mark Williams, and John Teasdale had all previously worked separately as researchers in the area of depression, and had made significant contributions to a CBT conceptualization of depressive episodes (Segal et al., 2002). In fact, before the project that led to the development of MBCT, Teasdale and Williams were both working at the same academic institution in Cambridge, UK. Each had developed their own theories regarding the dynamics and causes of depressive episodes, and they were each scheduled to present their research at an international conference in Oxford, England in 1989. They met before the conference to discuss some of the central research questions concerning how thoughts and emotions might contribute to depression. Their conversation at that time did not turn toward new treatment methods as much as it focused upon what styles of thinking and feeling might make a person more vulnerable to relapse and recurrence of depression (Segal et al., 2002).

In 1991 The John D. and Catherine T. MacArthur Foundation asked Zindel Segal to develop a "maintenance" method of cognitive therapy to address this very question of relapse and recurrence (Segal et al., 2002). As a result, Segal, Williams, and Teasdale met to begin development of just such a therapy modality in 1992. These meetings eventually led to the design, testing, and implementation of MBCT.

Segal, Williams, and Teasdale's collective analysis of the literature on depressive relapse vulnerability led them to hypothesize that a change in clients' relationship to their negative thoughts and feelings, through a process known as "de-centering," would be likely to help prevent relapse of depression. Understanding the concept of de-centering is central to understanding MBCT. Thus, in order to learn the MBCT model, we will examine the underlying background research and theory concerning depressive relapse and recurrence that has led to the theoretical foundations for MBCT. In doing this, we hope to get closer to the importance of de-centering, and to the unique character and flavor of MBCT.

THE NATURE OF DEPRESSION AND DEPRESSIVE RELAPSE

The Beckian cognitive model suggests that the experience of depressive episodes is caused by the activation of learned, "dysfunctional assumptions" (Beck et al., 1979). Dysfunctional assumptions are themselves the product of deeply held, somewhat nonconscious negative "core beliefs" that are learned early in life (Beck et al., 1979). Under the influence of stressful events, these underlying dysfunctional assumptions (e.g., "If I try to succeed, then I will certainly fail") are said to become "activated," producing "negative automatic thoughts" (Beck et al., 1979). In turn, these negative automatic thoughts cause destructive emotions and maladaptive behaviors that result in depression. In the original cognitive model, it is suggested that these dysfunctional assumptions exist as more or less static constructs, though they are only active under stressful conditions (Beck et al., 1979).

More recent research in CT has indicated that although dysfunctional assumptions do, indeed, appear elevated in persons with current depressive episodes, formerly depressed patients with a nondepressed current mood do not demonstrate any greater frequency or intensity of dysfunctional assumptions than do "never-depressed" research participants (Haaga, Dyck, & Ernst, 1991; Segal et al., 2002). Such studies effectively dismissed the idea that underlying, ongoing negative beliefs were likely to serve as the primary "trait-based," causal factors in depression.

Other research has suggested that a combination of cognitive factors, triggered under certain conditions, might better account for vulnerability to depressive relapse (Teasdale, Segal, & Williams, 1995). It appears that persons who are more vulnerable to depressive recurrence have repeatedly established mental relationships among depressed mood, negative cognitive predictions, and negative self-evaluative cognitions over their history of depressive episodes (Segal et al., 1996).

As a result, people with a history of depression are different from people who have never been depressed. However, this difference does not likely lie in the presence of an underlying pattern of cognitive content that *causes* depression, as in the original CT model. It seems that the difference may be better explained by the patterns of cognitions that are activated when a person experiences difficult emotions such as sadness and despair (Segal et al., 1996).

According to the line of thought that led to the development of MBCT, patients who have recovered from depression are vulnerable to a spiral of self-criticism and hopelessness when their life events lead them to experience negative emotions. So, if I am a person with a history of depression, I have had many experiences wherein sadness has become connected to negative thinking, uncomfortable physical sensations, and difficult life events over the course of my life. Any of these elements is so linked to the others in my mind, that stress at work might lead to deep sadness, then to a sense of myself as worthless, a hollow feeling in the pit of my stomach, and to staying in bed for days. These loops of depressive mental activity may be referred to as "self-perpetuating cycles of ruminative cognitive-affective processing" (Segal, Teasdale, & Williams, 2004, p. 48; Teasdale, 1988, 1997). Teasdale's (1997) work in particular points to an integrated pattern of cognitive processing that amounts to a holistic "mode of mind" that can be activated for previously depressed patients when they face stress and sadness. Physical sensations, emotions, memories, and emerging negative thoughts all converge in this mode to create a loop that initiates and perpetuates depression. This alternative cognitive model is supported by research on rumination and depressive relapse (Nolen-Hoeksema, 2000).

CENTRAL MBCT CONCEPTS AND TREATMENT RATIONALE

Traditionally, CT methods target change in the content of a depressed patient's cognitions. Cognitive therapists use systematic techniques to question the logic, utility, or validity of the depressed patient's thinking. For example, a cognitive therapist might teach patients to notice a negative automatic thought and to question the evidence for and against that thought. Patients are then trained to restructure their thinking into a more rational or functional alternative.

Despite the impressive outcome evidence for CT, we can't point to a large evidence base that suggests that cognitive therapy actually works *by* changing the content of the client's thoughts. As we have seen, dysfunctional attitudes alone do not seem to account for relapse of depression. As early as 1986, Hollon and Beck acknowledged that change in cognitive content may very well not be the active ingredient in cognitive therapy (Hollon & Beck, 1986). Subsequent component analyses of cognitive therapy have not proven that the cognitive challenging component of CT actually adds value to the therapeutic effectiveness of the overall therapy package (Longmore & Worrell, 2007).

As the field of CBT was beginning to come to terms with the fact that one of the most effective modes of CBT might not work in the way its theory suggested, other threads of intellectual discussion and inquiry were emerging throughout the CBT community. Teasdale's "Interacting Cognitive Subsystems Theory" (Barnard & Teasdale, 1991) and the work of Ingram and Hollon (1986) suggested that distancing and de-centering from negative cognitive content may, in fact, result in a change in clients' relationship to their depressing thoughts, emotions, and physical sensations.

This change in clients' relationship to their internal experiences might be more significant than direct change in cognitive content, according to this line of thought. Although this de-centering or distancing had always been a component of CT, it had not been put forward as a change process in the original Beckian model.

In the years preceding the development of MBCT, research on Dialectical Behavioral Therapy (DBT) (Linehan, 1993a) began to make a compelling case for the use of mindfulness training to help patients with borderline personality disorder. DBT employs mindfulness to teach patients to shift their perspectives on distressing mental experiences, as opposed to teaching direct cognitive change interventions. Mindfulness, as a part of skills training in DBT, appears to result in an improved capacity for emotion regulation and a reduction in self-injurious behaviors among people with borderline personality disorder (Linehan, 1993a). Acceptance and Commitment Therapy (ACT) also put forward a model in which a process known as "defusion" (S. C. Hayes et al., 1999) is said to help loosen the grip that negative cognitive content exerts on the behavior and experience of persons suffering from depression. Similarly, by the time MBCT was being developed, Kabat-Zinn's MBSR had already amassed the foundation of a research evidence base which suggested that mindfulness training may have a positive effect on clients' mood, quality of life, and levels of anxiety (Kabat-Zinn, 1990).

Based upon these growing trends in the research literature, their own collective research into the nature of vulnerability to depressive recurrence, and their own clinical experience, Segal, Williams, and Teasdale determined that an emphasis on de-centering may be important in the development of a cost-effective, time-limited group treatment for preventing depressive relapse (Segal et al., 2002). After a short while, they determined that mindfulness training might be an effective method for teaching clients such de-centering. This led to their adaptation of MBSR mindfulness training methods to the problem of depression, and their integration of mindfulness meditation with psychoeducational and theoretical elements of cognitive therapy.

According to MBCT training, when we are moving through our typical activities, pursuing goals, attempting to effect change on our environment, and pursuing objects in the world, we can be said to be acting in a "doing mode." Segal and colleagues (2002) write that this "doing mode" is a habitual mode of function, and we can really see it in action when our minds are dissatisfied with the reality we encounter. When we wish to have those things that we do not have, or wish to push away that which we do not want, our minds enter this "doing mode." Some negative feeling or craving is triggered, and our mind comes into action, drawing upon our habitual patterns of thinking, feeling, and behaving to achieve some object or change in state. Often, this is not a problem. We are thirsty, so we seek something to drink. We see an obstacle on our path, and we walk around it.

Sometimes, though, the discrepancy between how things are and how we would like them to be is more difficult to address. Perhaps the action that is called for is vague, or impossible. There may be an action we can take, but it isn't something we can do right now. In such cases, our "doing mode" doesn't really serve us.

Similarly, we are often troubled by our feelings or our thoughts. Naturally, our "doing mode" would suggest to us that we should take action. Often that action amounts to pushing away these thoughts, and attempting to avoid certain experiences. Throughout this book, we have seen that a great deal of research has established that attempts to treat our personal, internal experiences in this way can lead to more suffering (S. C. Hayes, Barnes-Holmes, Roche, 2001). When we attempt to push away feelings, thoughts, and mental events, they often are intensified and present themselves more frequently or strongly in our awareness (Wegner et al., 1987). In fact, the characteristics of this "doing mode" are often a lack of personal satisfaction, compulsively checking to see if we are anxious or sad, hurriedness in our daily tasks, compulsive self-criticism, and fruitless efforts to change what we just cannot change.

In MBCT, this tendency for human beings to lose themselves in habitual, goal-directed patterns, while remaining disconnected from an intentional awareness of the present moment, is also referred to as operating on "automatic pilot." When on "automatic pilot," we often apply this "doing mode" to our emotions. As a result, we can find ourselves in a ceaseless struggle to rid ourselves of unpleasant feelings that only serves to create an increasing wave of struggle and suffering.

Mindfulness presents us with a different option. In MBCT, the act of mindfully attending to our experience, moment-by-moment, is sometimes referred to as a "being mode." When in this "being mode," we are not completely wrapped up in the pursuit of specific goals or objects in the world. In the "being mode" we may find ourselves simply observing the stream of our consciousness, without judgment, evaluation, or even verbal description. By paying attention in this way, we may make a deeper contact with the present moment. The experience of mindfulness is said to involve an enhanced awareness, a greater clarity of perception, and an emerging spirit of willing acceptance of the whole of our reality, just as it is. By cultivating such a perspective, we may more fully experience the richness of what it means to be alive.

This distinction between the "doing" and "being" modes has some implications for how we might come to employ mindfulness in our everyday lives. Training in mindfulness is said to help us develop an *intentional* mode of awareness. We are deliberately moving our attention in a way that can involve both a disidentification from the contents of our conscious minds and a self-compassionate and nonjudgmental, full experience of our present moments (Segal et al., 2002). Although training in this mode of attention may begin on the meditation cushion or Yoga mat, a broader goal of mindfulness training is applying this type of attention to the act of living in the world, among others, on an ongoing basis.

Yongyey Mingyur Rinpoche (2007) has described mindfulness as "the key, the *how* of Buddhist practice [that] lies in learning to simply rest in a bare awareness of thoughts, feelings and perceptions as they occur" (p. 24). In recognizing the difficulties that clients may face in applying MBCT techniques, it is important to remember that applied mindfulness involves the ongoing development of a special way of paying attention to our experiences. This kind of attention is quite different from our typical, everyday way of attending to our lives.

Mindfulness represents a moment-by-moment observation of the unfolding flow of thoughts, feelings, and bodily sensations that presents itself within our consciousness, in real time, as we face whatever challenges and demands the world presents us with. We are invited to suspend our judgment of these experiences and to diligently, yet gently, draw our awareness, again and again, back to the flow of events in our consciousness. This intentional deployment of attention is engaged in and from the perspective of an engaged, yet dispassionate, observer. All of this is meant to be cultivated in the flow of life, rather than solely during formal training periods. This applied training in the generalization of mindfulness skills is an essential component of MBCT, and it is one of the ways that MBCT addresses depressive relapse.

OUTLINE OF THE MBCT PROGRAM

The MBCT group program is designed around an 8-week protocol. Groups meet once per week and last from 2 to 2½ hours. In addition to this series of meetings, participants in MBCT groups meet with a therapist for an assessment session, and for an orientation session before the group begins. Taking part in an MBCT group involves a commitment to maintain regular, daily mindfulness practice at home. Over the course of the 8 weeks, this practice might involve a range of exercises. Usually, the mindfulness homework involved in an MBCT group takes about 45 minutes per day.

Although MBCT is referred to as a group therapy, the structure is very different from a process-oriented therapy group. The emphasis of the meetings is placed upon the clients learning specific mindfulness practices and learning how to generalize and apply mindfulness in their daily lives. Much of the work involves experiential techniques and mindfulness meditations, which the group engages in together, in each session. MBCT sessions typically begin with a mindfulness meditation practice. These exercises vary over the course of the curriculum, but they may include a body scan, mindfulness of the breath, or a number of other guided meditation methods. Following an initial practice, the group is invited to discuss their week's experiences in applying and practicing MBCT methods. This is followed by the introduction of new practices, the discussion of a series of themes and concepts that relate to MBCT and depressive relapse, and the establishment of a new "homework" practice which will be undertaken over the course of the following week.

During the discussion and investigation periods that take place in MBCT groups, a certain characteristic conversational tone tends to emerge. This tone is consistent with a mindful, present-moment-focused awareness. Indeed, the style of inquiry and dialogue that is found in MBCT can be considered a form of applied mindfulness itself. The first stage in this inquiry period usually involves the facilitator of the group asking the participants to report whatever it is they noticed during their practice. In asking for what may have presented itself through the act of "noticing," the group leader isn't asking clients to analyze their experiences. The clients are encouraged to report upon their bare noticing of their direct experience. Often, the group leader will use reflective listening techniques to empathically summarize what clients have stated, rather than engaging in an intellectual interpretation of the clients' experiences.

After a period of time, when a number of the group's participants have had the opportunity to report upon what they have noticed, the MBCT group leader will ask questions that invite the participants to explore how their experience of mindfulness might differ from their everyday mode of paying attention. During this phase of the inquiry, clients are encouraged to relate their experience of mindfulness to the particular circumstances of their own lives. In doing so, they may draw distinctions between operating in a "doing mode" and a "being mode."

The third and final phase of discussion and inquiry invites the group to consider how their experiences and observations regarding mindfulness might be directly related to their aims in taking part in an MBCT course. For example, the facilitator might say the following: "Now that we've talked about what you've noticed during a week of practicing the body scan, I'm curious about something. How could our practice of directing attention around the body possibly help us to prevent depressive relapse?" During this period of inquiry, the participants may come to discover ways in which applied mindfulness can help them to de-center from depressing cognitive content, and how they might best take care of themselves. This process of inquiry is taught in residential MBCT teacher trainings, as is the entirety of the MBCT protocol. Rebecca Crane (2009) has delineated these three stages of the inquiry, and has labeled them as a "Noticing" step, a "Dialogue" step, and a final "Linking" step.

Each week of the MBCT program addresses a different theme, and presents the participants with particular exercises and homework practices (see Outline of the MBCT Program, pp. 62-63). The 1st week of MBCT training centers upon the theme of "Automatic Pilot." Clients are introduced to the concept of mindfulness, and how they might apply mindful awareness to break out of the habitual "automatic pilot" mode of relating to internal experiences and the world through rumination and experiential avoidance. As part of this 1st week, clients are taught the body scan, and their homework consists of a daily practice of this exercise.

Week 2 involves "Dealing with Barriers." After their 1st week of attempting regular engagement with a 45-minute-long guided mindfulness exercise, many clients will present with specific problems and obstacles that they have encountered. Therapists can expect a range of such barriers, including everything from "I couldn't stay awake during the exercise," to "I kept forgetting to schedule the body scan." The MBCT group leader adopts a validating and curious stance in response to these perceived obstacles. In session, a structured exercise in examining thoughts and feelings is typically used. This exercise foregrounds the ways in which our attachment to particular interpretations and analyses of our experience may take us out of contact with the present moment, and may carry us further into rumination and absorption in negative thinking.

Mindfulness of the Breath is the primary focus of the third MBCT session. During this group meeting, clients typically learn how to engage in a mindfulness of the Breath practice, as well as a Mindful Movement exercise. Mindful Movement is derived from Yoga postures, and it involves clients learning some of the most gentle and fundamental of such Yogic practices. This Yoga practice is not pursued as an end in itself. The postures are taught as a way of generalizing and deepening the client's practice and application of mindfulness. The 3rd week of MBCT training may also involve the use of a "Pleasant Events Calendar." This calendar is often given to clients in week 2, to be reviewed in week 3. Clients may use this worksheet to engage in the active, mindful noticing of events in their lives that bring them a sense of pleasure or satisfaction. This exercise, which is clearly adapted from CBT, can serve to blend mindful awareness, acceptance, and a deeper engagement with behavioral activation, to help prevent depressive recurrence. It is at this point in the protocol that clients learn an applied mindfulness exercise known as the "Three Minute Breathing Space." This practice will be described later in some detail, as an example of MBCT technique.

The 4th week of MBCT training centers on the theme of "Staying Present." During this meeting, the clients are invited to encounter ways in which mindfulness and acceptance may allow them to learn to remain in the presence of challenging emotional material. Rather than responding to depression through habitual avoidance or entanglement with negative automatic thinking, clients learn ways to directly experience thoughts, emotions and bodily sensations, while they take action to best take care of themselves in the present moment. The exercises that are taught and practiced in session include the Three Minute Breathing Space, applied as a tool for coping with stressful situations. Clients also begin to work with sitting meditation that expands mindfulness of breath to include mindfulness of the body, sounds, and mindfulness of thoughts themselves. As a sort of counterpoint to the Pleasant Events schedule from the previous week, clients often complete an Unpleasant Events Calendar between weeks 3 and 4. This provides a structured format for clients to rehearse bringing mindful acceptance to those aspects of life that they would most likely rather avoid.

Practicing acceptance and "allowing/letting be" is the focus of the 5th session of the MBCT protocol. The mindfulness exercises from the previous week, including the Three Minute Breathing Space and Mindfulness of Breath/Body/Sounds and Thoughts exercises, are rehearsed in session during this unit; however, the emphasis in the inquiry and discussion is placed upon cultivating willingness to meet unpleasant or difficult experiences with an attitude of "allowing." Clients are encouraged to cultivate an openness to letting things be as they are, while letting go of judgment and self-criticism. In the inquiry and discussion process, the group leader may attempt to help the clients to notice their habitual patterns of struggle, avoidance and rumination. Furthermore, the group may also serve to point out how the dominance of such patterns can make a person vulnerable to depression in the future.

Week 6 involves the theme "Thoughts Are Not Facts." In this session, clients work with perspective taking exercises that weave the concept of de-centering directly into their MBCT practice. At this point, the clients begin to take a close look at their own patterns of depressive relapse, and identify a "relapse signature," in the hopes that they may begin to develop an action plan to better respond to potential recurrences of depression. Mindfulness practices from earlier in the training are used, with an emphasis upon how we might best bring flexible and focused, intentional attention into contact with difficult thoughts and feelings. Throughout this session, clients and the therapist essentially engage in a practice of coming to terms with the way that negative thoughts may serve as a negative filter upon our moment-by-moment experience, enhancing the likelihood of depression. By accepting this process, observing it, and allowing thoughts to be just what they are, events in the mind, clients work to prepare themselves to prevent future relapse.

The 7th week of the MBCT program presents clients with the question of how they might adjust their day-to-day behavior to best prevent depression, and to cultivate self-care throughout their activities. The theme for this week's work is "How Can I Best Take Care of Myself?" In addition to mindfulness practices, participants in this session complete a list of all of their daily activities. After authoring this list, the clients are instructed to sort these activities into two categories. These categories are "nourishing" and "depleting." Clients are also asked to consider which activities in their lives provide them with a sense of pleasure and/or a sense of mastery. Over the course of this session, clients can again come into contact with their behavioral patterns, in a context of mindfulness and acceptance. Hopefully, clients will come to see that depression has some relationship to behavioral activation and self-care, as well as rumination and hanging out in the autopilot mode of attention. In this way, the central question, "How can I best take care of myself?" is made explicit, and the road to answers begins to be constructed.

In the final, 8th week of MBCT, clients are encouraged to acknowledge the completion of the group as the beginning of a new phase of their lives. The theme of this group is, "Using What Has Been Learned to Deal with Future Moods." This session usually involves some reflection upon how the clients may persist in bringing mindful awareness into their lives, in the absence of a structured program. The discussion in this week's group may also involve the relationship between the client's progress thus far in the program, and their use of mindfulness-based practices.

OUTLINE OF THE MBCT PROGRAM

Week	Theme	Important "In-Session" Content	Homework
1	**Automatic Pilot**	Raisin Exercise, Body Scan, Group formation	Daily 45-minute Body Scan, one mindful daily activity (such as brushing one's teeth mindfully)
2	**Dealing With Barriers**	Body Scan, Mindful Breathing, Mindfulness of Thoughts and Feelings	Daily 45-minute Body Scan, 10-Minute Mindful Breathing, Daily Record of Pleasant Events, new mindful daily activity
3	**Mindfulness of Breath**	Mindful Movement, Stretching with Mindful Breathing, Three Minute Breathing Space, Review of Pleasant Events Record	Mindful Movement, Mindful Stretching and Breathing, Daily Record of Unpleasant Events, Three Minute Breathing Space
4	**Staying Present**	A Sitting Meditation Involving: Mindfulness of Breath, Body, Sound, Thoughts, and Awareness Itself; Three Minute Coping Breathing Space, Mindful Walking, Review of Daily Record of Unpleasant Events	Sitting Meditation Involving: Mindfulness of Breath, Body, Sound, Thoughts, and Awareness Itself; Three Minute Breathing Space, Three Minute Coping Breathing Space
5	**Acceptance**	Sitting Meditation Involving: Mindfulness of Breath, Body, Sound, Thoughts, and Awareness Itself (with an emphasis upon noticing our reactions); Three Minute Breathing Space, Reading *The Guest House* poem by Rumi, Exploring habitual responding	Sitting Meditation Involving: Mindfulness of Breath, Body, Sound, Thoughts, and Awareness Itself; Three Minute Breathing Space, Three Minute Coping Breathing Space

Week	Theme	Important "In-Session" Content	Homework
6	**Thoughts Are Not Facts**	Sitting Meditation Involving: Mindfulness of Breath, Body, Sound, Thoughts, and Awareness Itself (with an emphasis upon noticing our reaction to a difficulty); Three Minute Breathing Space, Building a map of relapse signature and response plan, Alternative Perspective Taking Exercise	40 minutes per day of mindfulness practice drawn from the above central practices
7	**How Can I Best Take Care of Myself**	Examining the relationship between our behavioral patterns and our mental state (e.g., listing and noticing "nourishing" and "depleting" activities); Sitting Meditation Involving: Mindfulness of Breath, Body, Sound, Thoughts, and Awareness Itself (with an emphasis upon noticing our reactions); Three Minute Breathing Space	Developing a daily, personal practice based upon what has been learned; Developing and further elaborating a response plan to elements of depressive relapse
8	**Using What Has Been Learned To Deal With Future Moods**	Body Scan, Completion Meditation, Review and discussion of the entire course with an emphasis on the processes experienced and plans for future action to reduce vulnerability to depressive relapse and recurrence.	Development of 1-month personal practice plan

(Adapted from *Mindfulness Based Cognitive Therapy* [pp. 83-90] by R. Crane, 2009, London and New York: Routledge/Taylor & Francis. Adapted with permission.)

This brief outline of the structure of the MBCT program is meant to give you a "wide-angle" lens viewpoint on the major features of the therapy protocol in action. In order to take a closer look at the experiential flavor of MBCT techniques, we have provided a specific example of a mindfulness practice that is unique to MBCT.

EXAMPLE OF AN MBCT TECHNIQUE, "THE THREE MINUTE BREATHING SPACE"

MBCT has much in common with MBSR and other mindfulness-based therapies. It also does possess elements that are distinctive, as we have seen in our examination of MBCT's theoretical rationale. We would like to present an example of a clinical technique that is unique to MBCT, which is known as "The Three Minute Breathing Space" (Segal et al., 2002). This technique is based in the notion that mindfulness training is aimed at the development of a "real-time" change in the relationship between people and their thoughts and emotions. By bringing present-focused attention to the here and now, without judgment or analysis, we may be able to better come into contact with our mental events just as they are, not as the mind says they are.

One of the benefits of this kind of awareness is that it presents us with the opportunity to make decisions in the moment. When I realize that rumination and depressive thinking are beginning to unfold in my mind, I can choose to take action. I can choose to engage in self-care, to reach out to others in my support network, or even to simply make space for these experiences. In order to really apply mindfulness in the flow of life, it is clear that merely practicing a meditation exercise for 20 minutes, once a day, isn't likely to be sufficient. MBCT therapists are essentially aiming for their clients to bring mindfulness with them, as much as they can, in each step of their day-to-day lives. Developed by Segal and colleagues (2002), the "Three Minute Breathing Space" exercise is meant to teach the generalization of mindfulness skills.

This exercise is a part of the MBCT protocol, and it is taught in the 3rd week of the group therapy schedule (Segal et al., 2002). The therapist initially instructs the client to practice this mindfulness exercise three times a day, and then to apply it during situations that might call for de-centering, acceptance, and calm abiding. A transcript of an adapted version of the "Three Minute Breathing Space" (Segal et al., 2002) is included below.

THREE MINUTE BREATHING SPACE SCRIPT

As you learn this brief mindfulness practice, let's begin in a seated position. Later on, you might practice the "Three Minute Breathing Space" standing, sitting, and in many different situations, but for now, we will begin by sitting, and by allowing ourselves to fall silent and to fall still. Mindfulness is a quality of attention that is always available to us, even when we are not aware that we are available to it. To begin this practice, allow yourself to make whatever adjustments to your position that feel necessary. As we begin, we are consciously adopting a dignified, stable, and relaxed demeanor. Our backs are straight. We can feel ourselves grounded by the contact points where our bodies connect with the chair. Now, allow your eyes to close. Ask yourself, "What am I experiencing in this very moment?" "What do I feel in my body?" "What are my thoughts?" "What emotions am I feeling?" In this moment, we are paying attention even to those feelings, ideas, and sensations that may be experienced as unpleasant or upsetting. In doing so, we are allowing them to be just as they are. Allow yourself to make space for whatever is present, here and now.

Now, we are collecting our full attention and focusing it on the flow of our breath. Notice the subtle and more vivid changes in the body as the breath moves in and out. Breathing in, you know that you are breathing in. Breathing out, you know that you are breathing out. Take special notice of the flexible, flowing movement of the abdomen, as your body inhales and exhales. Stay with the flow of the breath, allowing your attention to blend with the movement of breathing itself, as best as you can, moment-by-moment.

In this moment, allow your awareness to expand to encompass the whole of your body. Bringing your attention into the body as a whole as you inhale, it is as if you are breathing attention itself into the body. As you exhale, completely let go of that awareness. It is as if your whole body is breathing, and softening around your experience. Stay with this experience for about a minute, allowing yourself to make space for whatever is present.

We now can begin to let go of this exercise, acknowledging that we have taken a few minutes to step out of automatic pilot, and to be present with our experience, directly, mindfully, and without judging.

SUMMARY

MBCT represents a turning point in the history of CBT. The methodical approach to outcome research, diagnosis-specific therapy methods, and the relationship to the cognitive model that are found in MBCT are all characteristic of the second generation of behavior therapies. However, the emphasis on mindfulness, acceptance, and self-compassion that permeates MBCT's approach is distinctly related to the third generation of behavior therapies that have been emerging over the course of the last 10 years.

MBCT represents a leap forward from a focus on methods that aim to directly change the content of a client's thoughts into a new mode of operation entirely. Mindfulness is used by MBCT practitioners to create an entirely new relationship between clients and the contents of their consciousness. Central to this relationship is a process known as "de-centering." This de-centering allows clients to move out of a "doing mode" and into a "being mode." From this vantage point, the ruminations and negative thoughts that herald the arrival of a depressive relapse no longer need to exert a controlling influence over clients' mood or behavior. In MBCT, mindfulness and a full, vivid acceptance of the present moment can provide clients with a working distance. This distance can allow our clients to learn to take care of themselves, to understand their patterns of potential depressive recurrence, and to embark upon lives lived more fully and with greater contact with the present moment, moment-by-moment.

FOR MORE INFORMATION

Segal, Z. V., Williams, J. M. G., & Teasdale, J. D. (2002). *Mindfulness-Based Cognitive Therapy for Depression: A New Approach to Preventing Relapse.* New York: Guilford Press. Known as the "green book," this text is a must read for anyone interested in MBCT. It covers the background and theory of MBCT, and covers in detail each of the eight sessions. It also includes client handouts.

Williams, M., Teasdale, J., Segal, Z., & Kabat-Zinn, J. (2007). *The Mindful Way Through Depression: Freeing Yourself from Chronic Unhappiness.* New York: Guilford Press.

Known as the "white book," this text is written more for lay audiences. It includes a CD with mindfulness exercises led by Jon Kabat-Zinn.

Mindfulness Based Cognitive Therapy – http://www.mbct.com/ This is the website of Zindel Segal, Mark Williams, and John Teasdale. It contains information and resources about MBCT.

Chapter 5

Dialectical Behavior Therapy

Dialectical Behavior Therapy (DBT) was developed by Marsha Linehan (1993a, 1993b) for use with individuals with Borderline Personality Disorder. DBT training involves a core component wherein clients are taught mindfulness to help with emotional regulation, and brief mindfulness exercises are used at the beginning of every group training session.

I (RWS) remember my very first exposure to DBT groups as an intern. I was very pleasantly surprised to hear the sound of a resonating bell at the beginning of each group, followed by a meditation exercise. I had almost left behind all my previous training in meditation when I went to graduate school, and felt like I was coming home when I discovered that my training could be put to use in the service of clients.

I also remember the intensity I experienced in some of the DBT groups. In the very first support group I attended, composed of graduates of the skills training groups, one of the members appeared very suicidal. The facilitator went around the room allowing each member to check in as to how the previous week had gone. One woman talked about how bad things were. She talked about writing her will and making funeral arrangements. She pulled up her sleeve and displayed her forearm, talking about the 20 razor cuts she had made. Her affect was very flat, and she spoke in a low, slow voice. I felt my heartbeat begin to increase as I mentally prepared myself for a crisis intervention. However, when the client finished speaking, the facilitator simply moved on to the next person. The group continued on with a multitude of topics, then came to a close after the 3 hours designated for the group had passed. I quickly rushed up to the facilitator and asked if we should have thought about hospitalizing her. She raised her eyebrows, smiled, and said, "Oh, she's doing much better this week."

This event, and my subsequent training in DBT, taught me a lot about how my own comfort level can get in the way of providing good services. Although working with individuals with borderline personality disorder can be very challenging, it can also be very rewarding. One of my colleagues really enjoys working with this population – she helps clients to channel all of their emotional chaos into a passion for life.

BORDERLINE PERSONALITY DISORDER

In looking over the *DSM-IV-TR* description of Borderline Personality Disorder (American Psychiatric Association, 2000), it is immediately obvious that these individuals have a lot of challenges. Individuals with this diagnosis have a long history of challenges involving a number of serious symptoms, such as trauma, abuse, fear of abandonment, emotional reactivity, unstable self-image, relationship instability, dissociation experiences, and self-mutilation and suicidal behaviors. Symptoms are often similar or overlapping with those of Posttraumatic Stress Disorder and/or Bipolar Disorder.

There is a great deal of stigma surrounding this diagnosis in the mental health field. Because these issues are so deep, and touch our own existential questions, clinicians are often unprepared to work effectively with this population. However, I found that often when I gave this diagnosis to someone, the client felt validated when I read the diagnostic criteria, as it put words to lived experiences.

Because this population struggles with mood instability, emotional dysregulation, and with dichotomous (black/white) thinking, a new approach was needed beyond what had been typically done in standard psychotherapy.

DEVELOPMENT OF DBT

In the 1970s, Marsha Linehan (1993a, 1993b) attempted to apply the principles of Cognitive-Behavioral Therapy (CBT) to the treatment of individuals with Borderline Personality Disorder. However, she found that traditional CBT's emphasis on change elicited resistance from her clients. She found that validation of the experiences and suffering of these individuals was helpful. From her knowledge of Eastern wisdom traditions, and her experience in practicing Zen, she taught the idea of "radical acceptance," that is, letting go of struggling against reality.

In helping clients balance change and acceptance, Linehan utilized the concept of dialectics. Dialectics involves the examination of opposing perspectives, often arriving at some type of integration or synthesis.

DBT emphasizes finding a balance between "reasonable mind" and "emotional mind," which Linehan calls "wise mind." When clients engage in dysfunctional behavior, a part of them recognizes that it is not helpful. They work to recognize and make more of their decisions from this wise part of themselves.

Linehan (1993a, 1993b) devised a skills training course consisting of four core modules: Core Mindfulness Skills, Interpersonal Effectiveness Skills, Emotion Regulation Skills, and Distress Tolerance Skills.

Each module meets once a week for 8 weeks. Though the entire training is 32 weeks long, new clients can enter at the beginning of any 8-week module. The first session of each module involves an overview of skills training (which can be abbreviated if there are no new members). The second session involves an overview of mindfulness skills. Sessions 3-7 are for the specific module skills. The last session is a review and provides an opportunity for good-byes for any members who have completed all the modules.

Linehan (1993b) lists three types of skills training procedures: (a) skills acquisition (when the skills are taught through instructions and modeling), (b) skill strengthening (such as through role plays and feedback), and (c) skill generalization (discussing how the material can be applied outside the group and giving the clients homework, which they record on diary cards).

STRUCTURE OF DBT

Dialectical Behavior Therapy is a multifaceted program. It is most effectively done using a team approach, in which the client receives individual therapy and participates in a skills training group. A member of the DBT team should be on call to handle crises between sessions. The crisis team member on call can utilize all of the skills the client is learning to help the client manage the emotional distress. The entire team meets regularly, ideally with a psychiatrist who is part of the team, to check in about how the clients are doing as well as to provide professional support to prevent burnout.

Because most crisis lines and emergency rooms are not adequately trained in DBT models, the on-call nurses can get very frustrated with repeated calls from clients and may discourage them from coming to the inpatient unit. Overwhelmed clients may then end up escalating with parasuicidal behaviors in order to feel heard and to get admitted to the hospital. Having an on-call DBT team member helps to circumvent this revolving door situation.

The skills training groups are designed to teach specific skills for dealing with distress, emotions, and relationships. The groups are relatively long (about 2-3 hours) in order to discuss the topics in depth, with an emphasis on applying the skills in daily life. In order to stay focused on the material, clients are discouraged from going into any depth about their own particular issues, and are encouraged to deal with those issues with their individual therapist.

Graduates of the skills training group may elect to go through the training again. Often, there is also an ongoing support group. When I (RWS) first sat in on one of the support groups during my internship training, I was amazed at how striking the difference was. In the skills group, clients are often new to the training, and frequently are dealing with emotional instability and distress. In the support group, some of the members had been attending for almost 10 years, and they described how they used the skills they had learned to effectively handle events in their personal lives. They were also good at giving and receiving support from each other.

DBT is described in detail in other works (e.g., Linehan, 1993a, 1993b) and requires quality training and supervision to do well. In this chapter, we will focus on the aspects of mindfulness and acceptance.

MINDFULNESS IN DBT

Mindfulness Skills is one of the four core modules in DBT group skills training, and is the only skill that is explicitly practiced throughout all of the training sessions. Concepts of mindfulness and acceptance are particularly helpful for a population that frequently engages in a lot of ruminations, judgments, and dichotomous thinking.

Linehan (1993b, p. 101) refers to mindfulness skills as "taking hold of your mind," a way of achieving "wise mind" by balancing "emotion mind" with "reasonable mind." Linehan breaks mindfulness down into "what" skills and "how" skills.

MINDFULNESS "WHAT" SKILLS

This aspect of the mindfulness training emphasizes observing, describing, and participating in moment-to-moment experiences as a way to reduce worries and ruminations. Observing helps facilitate the de-centering process, to reduce the emotional aversion to the experience. Describing also facilitates this state of awareness, and keeps attention on what is currently happening rather than going off into catastrophic thinking. Participating involves entering into activity completely – just as when you play a musical instrument, it seems to play itself, and if you think too much about it, you are likely to interfere with the process.

MINDFULNESS "HOW" SKILLS

This section of the training identifies the processes involved in mindfulness, which is done nonjudgmentally, one-mindfully, and effectively (Linehan, 1993b). Taking a nonjudgmental stance means to try to observe cause and effect without always automatically labeling people and events as "good" and "bad." One-mindfully means to do one thing at a time with all of one's attention. Effectively means to focus on what works in each situation.

MINDFULNESS IN SKILLS TRAINING GROUPS

DBT groups often start with a brief mindfulness exercise. This sets the tone for the group to be in a mindset of more openness and acceptance, as clients are often thinking about all the problems they may feel pressured to discuss.

Though not essential, a soothing bell tone is often used to wordlessly signal the beginning of the mindfulness exercise. The bell grabs one's attention, then gradually fades away, as a model for how thoughts can gradually become more quiet. Though group leaders may have different preferences, the bell can be struck three times to signal the beginning of the exercise. In formal practice, the first bell signals participants to settle in physically, the second tone reminds us to bring our minds to the present moment by focusing in on the breath, and the third peal signals the beginning of the exercise. A single tone signals the end of the exercise, reminding the clients to bring their awareness back to the group.

After the exercise, the clients are asked about their experience. The facilitators need to model the same type of mindfulness and acceptance that they are asking the clients to develop. Note in the example below that the therapist stays on process, not content:

Client: I tried to see the leaves floating in the water, but I kept thinking about what things are going to be like when I get home tonight.

Therapist: So you became aware that you kept thinking about your home, in the future. Were you able to bring your mind back to the image of the leaves?

Client: Yes, but I kept going right back to thinking about my boyfriend. I know he's going to yell at me tonight.

Therapist: So, you were able to keep bringing your mind back. The most important thing is to keep noticing where your mind goes, then to keep bringing it back. The more you practice, the easier it gets. Did you notice any sensations in your body when you noticed the thoughts about your boyfriend?

Client: Um, I'm not sure, I kept picturing him. I guess my stomach feels kinda tight.

Therapist: Did anyone else notice effects on your body when your mind was on other things?

It is important to keep mindfulness exercises short. Even 1 or 2 minutes can be productive, and 5 minutes can be more than enough. Traditional mindfulness exercises of 45 minutes will likely be impossible for everyone in the group to tolerate, because individuals with Borderline Personality Disorder are often struggling with emotional dysregulation. Too much silence may also bring up past traumas, which is very challenging to handle adequately in a group setting.

There are many different types of mindfulness exercises. By practicing a variety of methods, clients may find certain ones that work best for them. It is important to keep the exercises short and structured, without too much silence, especially if there are new members in the group.

The mindfulness exercises are intended for clients to better understand how their minds work and to teach them to better tolerate their emotions without acting out in unhealthy ways. Roemer and Orsillo (2009) describe an exercise used in DBT that exemplifies the kinds of exercises that are useful. Clients are guided in a visualization exercise in which one imagines that one's mind is the sky, and that one's thoughts and feelings are clouds floating by. Clients are encouraged to continually place their thoughts onto the clouds, and to watch them drift on, rather than getting caught up in them. By doing this, the goal is for the clients to identify more with their minds as the context in which thoughts and feelings arise and pass away.

A similar exercise can be done using a conveyor belt, on which buckets are moving past, having the clients imagine dumping their thoughts into the buckets as they are carried away. S. C. Hayes et al. (1999) use similar images, such as imagining thought trains speeding past, or leaves floating down a stream.

Rizvi, Welch, and Dimidjian (2009) give examples of exercises to develop wise mind, to observe, to describe, and to participate:

Wise Mind

Ask clients to follow the feeling and cadence of their breath with a simple practice, or whatever practice has already been learned. After a few moments, ask clients if they can experience or connect with a wise, centered place within them.

Observe

The therapist can bring in something small to eat like a raisin, piece of fruit, mint, or small chocolate. Clients are asked to observe the sensations of eating, such as taste, texture, smell, and the physical sensation of swallowing.

Describe

Following an observe exercise like the one above, clients can be asked to describe their experience, without adding on judgments, interpretations, and so forth.

Participate

Any activity that prompts self-consciousness offers abundant opportunity for practicing the skill of participate. Popular choices include singing (e.g., typical rounds such as "Row Row Row Your Boat"), dancing, or laughing out loud in a "laugh club."

(Abridged from "Mindfulness and Borderline Personality" by S. L. Rizvi, S. S. Welch, & S. Dimidjian, in *Clinical Handbook of Mindfulness* [Edited by F. Didonna; pp. 255-256], 2009, New York: Springer. Copyright © 2009 by Springer Science + Business Media B.V. Reprinted with kind permission from Springer Science + Business Media B.V.)

ACCEPTANCE
IN DBT

As discussed in Chapter 1, mindfulness and acceptance are very interrelated. Mindfulness is about "turning toward" and courageously looking at what is.

Because the concept of acceptance in common use implies that what happened is okay, and is so difficult for an individual who has suffered a great deal of trauma or abuse, the term "radical acceptance" is used in DBT (Brach, 2003; Linehan, 1993a, 1993b).

As in other therapies, it is very important to balance empathy for a client's pain and suffering with the idea of acceptance. Radical acceptance helps to counterbalance the many judgments of self and others. Much energy is wasted wishing things were other than they are or were, particularly when you have suffered horrible abuses over a lifetime. However, by first accepting reality as it is, one can move forward to make changes.

In her client video on reality acceptance, Linehan (2005) states that though there may be an infinite variety of painful experiences you can have, there are only four responses you can make:

1. You can solve the problem.
2. You can change how you feel about the problem.
3. You can accept the problem.
4. You can stay miserable.

Because so many individuals with Borderline Personality Disorder have experienced significant past abuse, options 1 and 2 are difficult or impossible. Most choose option 4. DBT focuses most on option 3.

There are three parts to the reality acceptance skills taught by DBT: radical acceptance, turning the mind, and willingness (Linehan, 1993a, 1993b, 2005).

RADICAL ACCEPTANCE

Linehan (2005) defines the "radical" in radical acceptance as "complete and total," as when you let go of the fight with reality. It is complete acceptance with both body and mind. She notes that suffering is pain paired with nonacceptance. The goal is not to take away all pain (which would be impossible), but to do what you can to turn suffering into ordinary pain.

Linehan (1993a, 1993b, 2005) describes three parts of radical acceptance. The first is accepting that reality is what it is. Reality must be accepted before it can be changed – acceptance does not mean that you like or approve of the way things are. As Linehan (2005) notes, it is easy to accept good things. The higher the level of pain involved, the harder it is to accept things.

The second part of radical acceptance is accepting that everything has a cause (Linehan, 1993a, 1993b, 2005). This provides an alternative to wallowing in "Why me?" or "Things should not be the way they are." Because everything comes about from a cause, from a certain perspective, everything is as it should be. Even if you don't know what the cause is, you can accept that there is a cause. This also opens up the possibility that new causes can create new outcomes.

The third part of radical acceptance is accepting that life can be worth living, even with painful events in it (Linehan, 1993a, 1993b, 2005). No one is free from pain in life. If you spend too much time complaining about the pain, and wait for the pain to go away before moving on with life, nothing will ever happen. One can live a happy and productive life even though painful things do happen.

TURNING THE MIND

The next part of reality acceptance is called "turning the mind" (Linehan 1993a, 1993b, 2005). Radical acceptance is not something you do once and for all – you have to practice doing it over and over. Throughout the day, we have to make a conscious choice to turn our minds toward acceptance.

Linehan (2005) outlines three steps in turning the mind. The first is to mindfully be aware of when you are not accepting. Frequently, this will be experienced as anger, bitterness, feeling that life is unfair, and in trying to escape reality. The second step is to make an inner commitment to accept, knowing that even though it is difficult, resisting or denying reality will only make things harder. The third step is to turn the mind toward acceptance over and over and over again.

WILLINGNESS

Willingness involves the attitude or stance you take, allowing the world to be as it is. It is a commitment to active involvement in life. It includes the realization that you are a part of and connected to life (Linehan, 2005).

The opposite of willingness is willfulness – refusing to be part of life, trying to deny, ignore, or push away our experiences. Linehan (2005) recommends four things to do when willfulness shows up. The first is simply to notice that it is there; to observe that it has arisen. The second is to radically accept that willfulness is present. The third is to make a conscious decision to turn your mind toward acceptance and willingness. The fourth is to try to assume a willing posture, such as opening your hands and arms, and saying "yes" to your experiences.

As Linehan (2005) notes, the above suggestions take everyone a lifetime of practice. No one is always accepting of reality. The way to begin is to practice on small things first, then gradually develop the habit of noticing when resistance arises, and remembering to mindfully observe what is present.

INDIVIDUAL APPROACHES WITH DBT

Though designed as a comprehensive, multifaceted intervention, DBT techniques are sometimes utilized with individual clients. Because a client usually needs all the time in individual therapy to discuss ongoing life crises, Linehan (1993b) states that "trying to conduct skills training with a borderline individual is like trying to teach a person to put up a tent in the middle of a hurricane" (p. 9). It is very challenging to treat an individual with borderline personality disorder without the comprehensive system, but clinicians in rural areas, especially in agencies with limited funding, may have little choice.

The client handouts from Linehan's skills training manual (1993b) can be very useful in working with individual clients. The interpersonal effectiveness concepts are particularly useful, even for individuals without a diagnosis of Borderline Personality Disorder.

Of course, one must be careful when using DBT techniques outside of the context in which they were developed. It is important to receive training in the full DBT program before attempting to implement specific techniques with individual clients. Further research needs to be done to evaluate the best way to use these techniques individually.

CASE EXAMPLE: MARY

I (RWS) once utilized DBT mindfulness techniques with an individual client who was suffering from PTSD. The client was a female of European ancestry, whom we will call Mary. She was referred to her Employee Assistance Program for anxiety, which was interfering with her work. She was a quality inspector, and her difficulty concentrating could have endangered the lives of the company's customers. Mary had suffered significant sexual abuse from her stepfather growing up. As is common in such cases, her mother did not believe it and made threats to Mary not to talk about it. When it finally came out into the open, the stepfather went to prison for a year. However, when the stepfather was released from prison, he returned to live in the house again, as if nothing had ever happened.

Mary did her best to suppress all the psychological consequences of her abuse. However, as she grew older, she found this increasingly difficult to do. She saw a flyer for a sexual abuse survivor support group and decided to attend a meeting. Unfortunately, it was a self-help group, and there were no professionals present to ease new members into the process. Members began describing their past experiences very openly, and sometimes graphically. Mary immediately began having flashbacks of her own experiences, and she could not control them in the days that followed, interfering with her work.

Mary was too distressed to even begin to imagine talking about the actual abuse, and would not even consider using the "screen" technique. The screen technique involves imagining that you are watching the traumatic events taking place on a giant movie theatre screen in front of you, helping you to de-center from the emotional impact of the traumatic event (because during flashbacks, clients feel that they are back in the traumatic situation again, triggering all the physiological reactions).

Operating in crisis intervention mode, I utilized the distress tolerance skills of DBT. From the mindfulness skills component, we practiced using the "bucket/conveyor belt" technique, which she found helpful. As I worked with her to reduce her emotional distress, I told her that she was at a crucial point – she could either stuff it back down again, or engage in long-term therapy to process all of the past trauma she had endured. Fortunately, she chose the latter.

USE OF DBT IN PSYCHIATRIC
EMERGENCY ROOMS

Sneed, Balestri, and Belfi (2003) describe the use of DBT in psychiatric emergency rooms. One of the primary goals in an acute crisis unit is to engage the client in long-term outpatient treatment. Too often, patients come for help with their acute stress, but don't adequately address the underlying issues, resulting in a "revolving door" situation. The article by Sneed and colleagues (2003) is divided into four sections, describing strategies and techniques from DBT designed to foster readiness for change in the client.

Validation

Because parasuicidal clients are experiencing a lot of chaos, it is important to validate their feelings and experiences to develop a working alliance. This sets the foundation for acceptance. Linehan (1997) and Sneed et al. (2003) outline six levels of validation, each subsequent one encompassing those before it:

1. Focus on listening and observing.
2. Focus on accurate reflection.
3. Interpret (articulate an understanding of the client's worldview).
4. Focus on the causes of behavior given client's life history.
5. Acknowledge history but point out detrimental consequences of maladaptive behavior.
6. Radical genuineness (seeing client as an equal, with strengths and vulnerabilities, and believing in client's potential).

Extending and the devil's advocate technique

Sneed et al. (2003) discuss extending and the devil's advocate technique as the two primary strategies for connecting emergency room patients with outpatient treatment. "Extending" means taking a patient's position to a further extreme than they themselves intend (Linehan, 1993a). For instance, a patient who is told by the ER staff that she can go home after only an overnight stay may feel that she is not taken seriously. She may mumble to the therapist that she will end up cutting herself again, expecting the therapist to downplay the seriousness of this. If the therapist says, "I'm really concerned when I hear you say that – let me see if there is a way we can get you admitted to the inpatient unit for a month," the patient is likely to be more open to committing to outpatient therapy.

Similarly, the "devil's advocate technique" is meant to counterbalance a patient's extreme views by taking the opposite view (Linehan, 1993a). Linehan (1993a) and Sneed et al. (2003) use the example of a therapist discouraging therapy for a treatment-resistant patient. By taking an extreme position of how difficult the therapy process will be, it will invoke a desire in the patient to argue for reasons that he or she should do therapy.

As with any paradoxical intervention strategies, these techniques must be used with caution.

Irreverent communication

DBT promotes a strategy known as "irreverent communication" Linehan (1993b). Clients often expect therapists to be overly serious and "stuffy," so therapists can counteract this by poking fun of themselves and the client's behavior. By light-heartedly teasing clients about their maladaptive behavior ("So, after taking 50 pills, you just knew the whole world would stop and apologize to you?"), or by becoming overly enthusiastic about their adaptive behavior ("Fantastic! You actually asked for what you wanted! It only took you 30 years to figure out people can't read your mind!"), clients can be jolted into seeing things from a new perspective, in which they can take themselves less seriously.

Linehan says that this can be tricky in a group setting, as the facilitator must monitor the responses of each individual to make sure the irreverent communication is received in the right way. Hence, this approach is better suited to individual work.

Sneed et al. (2003) describe the use of the irreverent communication strategies known as *plunging* and *confrontation*. Plunging involves being very direct, which the patient often finds refreshing. Confrontation challenges the patient's dysfunctional behavior. "So, did this suicide attempt get you the results you wanted?" Again, these techniques must be applied carefully, monitoring the patient's response and repairing any damage done to rapport.

The good clinician/bad clinician technique and the use of metaphor

Linehan (1993a, 1993b) describes the use of the "good guy versus bad guy" strategy in DBT groups. One clinician (the "good" one) works to build empathy with the client in order to keep him or her engaged in therapy. The other clinician (the "bad" guy) enforces the rules and is more challenging with the client.

Sneed et al. (2003) have used this technique in the emergency room, as a way of bringing out the patient's own ambiguous feelings about how to proceed. One clinician can validate the extreme chaos in the patient's life, and the other can be more challenging about how dangerous the patient's behavior is, and how it needs to change.

The use of metaphor is common in therapy, and very useful in DBT as a simple image for a client's complex emotions (Linehan, 1993a, 1993b). Sneed et al. (2003) find metaphors particularly helpful in emergency rooms, because they can help the client feel validated and are easier to understand than cognitive interpretations. After listening to a patient describe the chaos that preceded a suicide attempt, a clinician can say, "It sounds like you were barely hanging on to the edge of a cliff, and decided it was easier to just let go. But you've survived the fall, and now we need to figure out how to help you climb back out of this abyss."

OTHER APPLICATIONS OF DBT

Though originally designed for the treatment of Borderline Personality Disorder, DBT is now being used in a variety of settings for a range of presenting issues.

In their book on extending the applications of DBT, Dimeff, Koerner, and Linehan (2007) present chapters on inpatient units (Swenson, Witterholt, & Bohus, 2007), adult and juvenile residential forensic settings (McCann et al., 2007), eating disorders (Wisniewski, Safer, & Chen, 2007), families (Fruzzetti, Santisteban, & Hoffman, 2007), adolescents (A. L. Miller et al., 2007), depression and older adults (Lynch & Cheavens, 2007), and assertive community treatment (ACT) teams (Reynolds et al., 2007). They also include a chapter on evaluating DBT programs (Rizvi, Monroe-DeVita, & Dimeff, 2007).

Linehan and her colleagues have also found success in utilizing DBT with individuals with dual diagnoses of Borderline Personality Disorder and substance dependence (Linehan et al., 1999; McMain et al., 2007).

Other applications of DBT skills include anxiety disorders (Gratz, Tull, & Wagner, 2005), depression and anxiety (Marra, 2004), couples therapy (Fruzetti, 2006), parenting (Harvey & Penzo, 2009), bipolar disorder (Van Dijk, 2009), binge eating and bulimia (Safer, Telch, & Chen, 2009), and treatment of suicidal adolescents (A. L. Miller, Rathus, & Linehan, 2006).

EMPIRICAL SUPPORT

Dialectical Behavior Therapy for Borderline Personality Disorder is listed on the APA Division 12 website of research-supported psychological treatments as having "strong research support" (Society of Clinical Psychology [n.d.]).

The Behavioral Tech Web site (2010)* summarizes the major research on DBT:

Two randomized controlled trials (RCTs) of DBT . . . have indicated that DBT is more effective than Treatment-As-Usual (TAU) in treatment of BPD and treatment of BPD and co-morbid diagnosis of substance abuse (Linehan, Armstrong, Suarez, Allmon & Heard, 1991; Linehan, Schmidt, Dimeff, Craft, Kanter & Comtois, 1999). Clients receiving DBT, compared to TAU, were significantly less likely to drop out of therapy, were significantly less likely to engage in parasuicide, reported significantly fewer parasuicidal behaviors and, when engaging in parasuicidal behaviors, had less medically severe behaviors. Further, clients receiving DBT were less likely to be hospitalized, had fewer days in hospital, and had higher scores on global and social adjustment. Likewise, in the RCT . . . for women with co-morbid substance abuse, in addition to similar findings to the original study regarding improvement in BPD criterion behaviors, DBT was more effective than TAU at reducing drug abuse. Follow up indicated that subjects who had received DBT also had greater gains in global and social adjustment . . . Koons, Robins, Tweed & Lynch (2001) randomly assigned 20 women veterans diagnosed with BPD to either DBT or TAU. Unlike Linehan's, et al. (1991, 1993) original studies, subjects were not required to have a recent history of parasuicide. However, subjects enrolled in DBT showed statistically significant reductions in suicidal ideation, depression, hopelessness, and anger . . . . Verheul, Van Den Bosch, Koeter, De Ridder, Stijnen & Van Den Brink (2003) conducted an RCT in the Netherlands, again comparing DBT to TAU. Their findings are consistent with the earlier studies. . . .

*From http://www.behavioraltech.com/resources/whatisdbt.cfm. Reprinted with permission.

A more recent study (Linehan et al., 2006) involved a 1-year RCT and a 1-year posttreatment followup of DBT versus treatment by experts. Those in the DBT group had better overall outcomes, were half as likely to make suicide attempts, and spent less time in the hospital.

Ongoing research is being done to measure the effectiveness of DBT for other presenting concerns.

DEVELOPING COMPETENCE

Fortunately, those clinicians who want to gain competence in using DBT have several options available to them. There are now a multitude of books, videos, organizations, training opportunities, and consultants available.

A good place to begin is to get involved with Marsha Linehan's organization, Behavioral Tech, LLC (http://www.behavioraltech.org). The website sells books, videos, and mindfulness audio CDs by Dr. Linehan and others. It also offers online and in-person training courses in all four DBT skills modules.

Clinicians who are serious about learning DBT may also benefit from joining the Dialectical Behavior Therapy Association (DBTA), which is a part of PESI, LLC. For more information, visit http://www.pesi.com/dbta/.

Of course, the best way to learn DBT is by working under supervision in an agency with experienced DBT facilitators.

FOR MORE INFORMATION

Linehan, M. M. (1993). *Cognitive-Behavioral Therapy for Borderline Personality Disorder.* New York: Guilford Press.

Linehan, M. M. (1993). *Skills Training Manual for Treating Borderline Personality Disorder.* New York: Guilford Press.

(Linehan's original book, and the companion skills training manual, are required reading to understand the theoretical foundations of DBT. The skills training manual outlines all of the groups and provides client handouts.)

Chapter 6

Acceptance and Commitment Therapy

As mindfulness practices have had an increasing influence upon Western psychotherapies, many variations in their application have evolved. Acceptance and Commitment Therapy (ACT) has emerged over the course of the last 20 years as one of the fastest growing areas of clinical and research interest in mindfulness and cognitive-behavioral therapies. As we begin to take a closer look at ACT, it is worth noting that, when spoken out loud, ACT is pronounced as the word "act" rather than as a series of letters, like "ay see tea." This reflects the particular emphasis upon taking action toward valued directions that is found in this form of psychotherapy. This importance placed upon behavior change makes sense, because mindfulness-based work in ACT gradually developed from a global research initiative that has its roots in the methodology of the radical behaviorist tradition, rather than a simple grafting of Buddhist techniques onto existing therapy methods.

In ACT, the definition of mindfulness involves several central, interacting behavioral processes (S. C. Hayes et al., 1999). These processes blend with one another to allow for a flexible, focused attention to the present moment (Wilson & DuFrene, 2008). This mode of attention also involves letting go of literalized interpretations of mental phenomena, and an emergent willingness to experience the unfolding flow of our conscious experiences without judgment or needless defenses. Beyond this, mindfulness in ACT also evokes a transcendent sense of self, which can effectively break our overidentification with our stories about our past and future. If all of this seems a little complicated at this point, perhaps we can take a deep, mindful breath and just make space for that sense of confusion.

In order to best understand an ACT-consistent perspective on mindfulness, and how to use that perspective to help alleviate suffering, it is best to take a little time to review the underlying basics of ACT theory and practice. The following sections will review the foundations of ACT. As we walk through the processes that ACT identifies and targets, we will examine clinical examples that illustrate how these processes can be worked within an actual psychotherapy situation. It is important to remember that the processes we are discussing apply to both therapists and patients. The act of coming into the present moment, letting go of attached and habitual perspectives, and opening to all of what life has to offer is a shared process that unfolds throughout the course of therapy, as it does over the course of a lifetime.

PHILOSOPHICAL FOUNDATION

One of the distinctive characteristics of ACT is that it is explicitly based upon a particular philosophy of science. Although many schools of psychotherapy have implied philosophies, ACT is one of the only forms of therapy that grounds itself in one specific philosophy. This adherence to a philosophical foundation relates to the origins of ACT within the tradition of behavior analysis. Some of the language involved in behavioral analysis can sound rather tricky at first. However, with a little time and patience, it can become clear that the concepts are actually far simpler than they seem.

The philosophy that underlies behavior analysis is known as *Functional Contextualism* (S. C. Hayes et al., 1999). This is an American pragmatic philosophy, which is often described as "a-ontological." This just means that Functional Contextualism doesn't claim to say anything about what is "absolutely true" or "real" in the universe. It is merely a way of talking about the world around us and how we interact with it, without asserting that these observations are *the* literal, final word about what really "is." From this perspective, there is room for the abundant value found in the range of other philosophies, religious traditions, and even poetry and the arts. We humans have developed many ways of describing our experience and our world, after all. Functional Contextualism is a way of understanding our interactions with our environment in the context of behavioral science.

Within a Functional Contextualist system, "truth" represents whatever works to allow for prediction and influence of a person's behavior in the service of his or her freely chosen, valued directions (Biglan & S. C. Hayes, 1996; S. C. Hayes et al., 2001). This pragmatic and contextual sense of what is "true" allows therapists and researchers to pursue techniques that allow clients to broaden their range of available behaviors, even in the presence of disturbing or unwanted thoughts and feelings. This expansion of the range of possible behaviors isn't thought of as an end in itself. Within ACT, a broadening behavioral repertoire is sought in the service of people moving toward those aspects of life that increase a sense of meaning, vitality and purpose for them.

It's important to point out that when Functional Contextualists discuss behavior, they don't just mean what we can observe organisms doing. In the behaviorist tradition, "behavior" is defined as anything and everything that an organism does, from "private events" like thinking, feeling, and daydreaming to "public events" such as walking, talking, or throwing a softball. Behavior analysts seek to understand the current and historical influences on a person's behavior. In doing so, they aim to develop reliable and precise strategies that can help to shape more workable and adaptive behaviors.

THEORY OF LANGUAGE AND COGNITION

In addition to having a foundation in a specific school of philosophy, ACT is also based upon a particular behaviorist theory of language and cognition, known as Relational Frame Theory (RFT; S. C. Hayes et al., 2001). RFT attempts to use scientifically validated principles of learning theory to explain and understand the most fundamental aspects of human language and thought. As a part of this, applied RFT also provides explanations for the processes that are involved in human suffering and psychopathology (S. C. Hayes et al., 2001).

According to RFT, the central cause of psychological problems involves the ways in which the nature of language contributes to "experiential avoidance" (S. C. Hayes et al., 2004; Luoma, S. C. Hayes, & Walser, 2007). Experiential avoidance represents a person's efforts to control or alter the form, frequency, or situational sensitivity of thoughts, feelings, and sensations, even when doing so causes behavioral harm (S. C. Hayes et al., 1996). A reasonable person might ask, "Why should experiential avoidance be the prime mover in psychopathology? I get that avoidance is involved in learning anxious behaviors, but what leads it to be *so* important in this model?" If we scratch the surface of RFT a little bit more, we can quickly find our answers.

According to RFT, humans learn to relate events and experiences to one another in a developing "relational network" over the course of their lives. This process is called "derived relational responding." As a result, we learn to respond to events based, in part, on their relationship to other events, and not just based on the properties of the event at hand (S. C. Hayes et al., 2001). In this way, one event may come to be related with any other event.

Here's an example. Let's imagine that you once attended a wonderful birthday party that was thrown for you by many good friends and family. All of your loved ones were gathered there to honor you, at a fine restaurant. When you were asked to make a speech, you accidentally slipped when rising from your chair, spilling red wine all over your new yellow dress, stumbling onto the cake, and swearing out loud in the process. You still can recall the laughter of the guests and the sense of humiliation you felt as you hurried to clean yourself off in the restroom. In the future, what might pop into your head and arise in your heart if you heard that a party was being thrown in your honor? Might you feel a little twinge of dread or embarrassment when you passed by that particular restaurant? The experience of a birthday party or that restaurant has now been indelibly *related* to the experience of shame and embarrassment. Such relations tend to stick around once they are established. When we hear "*Mary had a little . . .*" doesn't our mind immediately offer up the word "*lamb?*" Our personal history is the history of building this relational network, from an RFT perspective.

RFT also suggests that when we experience thoughts or mental representations of an event, the stimulus properties of such an event show up in a literalized fashion. So, when a person with depression experiences the negative thought, "I am a worthless person," he or she responds emotionally to this sentence as though it were real and literal. The fact that this verbal evaluation is not reality itself, and is actually just an event in the mind, doesn't seem to factor into the equation at that point. RFT describes the process of experiencing mental events as though they were literal as "cognitive fusion" (S. C. Hayes et al., 1999).

Given the processes of derived relational responding and cognitive fusion, we find ourselves in a troubling situation. By virtue of the way language works, we can learn to relate any event to any other. To make matters more complicated, when a mental representation of an event is triggered, we may respond to the stimulus properties of that mental representation as though it were literal. This context of literality, if you will, causes our distressing thoughts and feelings to exert a narrowing influence on our range of behavior, just like actual aversive events in the world might.

It's clear how this situation might involve some psychological pain, but the dynamics of human suffering and experiential avoidance involve a few more steps before the situation becomes completely clear.

Human beings have been designed by evolution to try to avoid or escape dangerous situations in the outside world. For example, if my genetic predecessor of a million years ago came to fear that a certain watering hole was dangerous, he probably avoided it. In doing so, he was that much less likely to be snatched up by the lurking prehistoric crocodile just beneath the surface of the water. This strategy of avoidance of aversive or dangerous things in the outside world is a hard-won evolutionary feature of human beings.

Unfortunately, this strategy of avoidance can backfire when it is applied to our thoughts, emotions, and mental representations. According to RFT, when we attempt to avoid, suppress, or eliminate unwanted mental events, we might experience these events more frequently or intensely (S. C. Hayes et al., 1999). This is easy to comprehend, in that trying to "not think about depression" involves, by definition, thinking about depression. Experimental research has famously demonstrated that the more we try to suppress thinking of something, the more we tend to think about it (Wegner et al., 1987; Wenzlaff & Wegner, 2000). For example, if we were asked to "not think of a purple Volkswagen" for the next 5 minutes, how often do you think that purple Beetle would pop up in our mind's eyes? It seems that whatever we aren't willing to experience, we are destined to experience.

Thus, the nature of human language and cognition leads us to a very tricky situation. It is our nature to mentally relate experiences in our environment and in our minds to other experiences, which means that all sorts of situations can trigger potentially unwanted thoughts, feelings and images. When these mental events show up, we often experience them as though they were literal, with our minds and bodies responding with anxiety or distress. To make matters that much worse, the more we try to escape or avoid these experiences, the more they show up.

The situation at this point can seem rather bleak. Nevertheless, as we know, human language, emotion and cognition is far more than a curse. In fact, it also can be viewed as a blessing that has allowed our species to flourish, advance, and evolve into a fascinatingly complex and important aspect of life on Earth. Perhaps the crux of the problem of human suffering lies in the nature of human language, but this may also be where we find the solution to liberation from suffering.

PSYCHOLOGICAL FLEXIBILITY AND THE HEXAFLEX

ACT provides a model of mental wellness that is central to the aims of psychotherapeutic interventions, and this model is known as "psychological flexibility" (S. C. Hayes & Smith, 2005). Psychological flexibility may be defined as "the ability to contact the present moment more fully as a conscious human being, and based on what the situation affords, to change or persist in behavior in order to serve valued ends" (Luoma et al., 2007, p. 17; S. C. Hayes & Smith, 2005). There are six core processes which are believed to contribute to psychological flexibility, and these processes are often illustrated in a visual diagram known as a "hexaflex" (see Figure 1, p. 91) (S. C. Hayes, Luoma, et al., 2006). These six processes work together in an interactive way to bring clients into direct experiential contact with their present moment experiences, to disrupt cognitive fusion, to promote experiential acceptance, to help clients let go of attachment to their narrative construction of themselves, to assist clients in the process of values authorship, and to facilitate clients' commitment to valued directions in their lives. In the following sections, we will take a much closer look at these processes, one at a time, using clinical examples to help illustrate what actually happens in the consultation room when an ACT therapist is helping a patient to move toward psychological flexibility. As we will see, throughout the course of ACT, patients gradually learn to expand their behavioral repertoire in the presence of distressing internal events, through cultivating mindful awareness, acceptance, and committed action toward what matters most to them. The first four core processes, which include Contact with the Present Moment, Defusion, Acceptance, and Self as Context, are the four operational elements that blend to result in a state of mindfulness, from an ACT-consistent point of view. As a result, we will begin our discussion of the hexaflex elements with these four mindfulness-oriented processes.

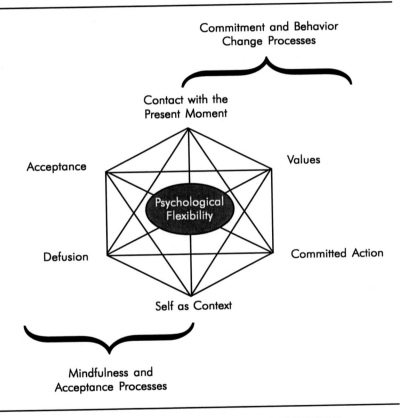

FIGURE 1: THE HEXAFLEX; MINDFULNESS PROCESSES
(Reprinted with permission, courtesy of Kelly Wilson and Steven C. Hayes.)

CONTACT WITH
THE PRESENT MOMENT

The first ACT process we will examine is known as "Contact with the Present Moment." ACT encourages clients to be present to external and internal events, as much as they can, moment-by-moment, in a nonjudgmental fashion. This focus on the ongoing process of experience, as it unfolds in the mind, serves to bring clients into direct contact with the conscious, fully awake action of simply being alive, as opposed to habitual immersion in imaginal constructions of possible futures or remembered pasts.

The quality of attention that is brought to the present moment can be described as flexible and focused (Wilson & DuFrene, 2008). Flexible attention allows individuals to shift their awareness as needed to the elements of their environment and inner world that require attention in order to pursue valued aims. Additionally, focused attention draws our awareness back from distractions and the many natural, yet unhelpful, wanderings of the mind, so that we may bring all of who we are to bear upon the things that matter.

This contact with the present moment is achieved by simply noticing what is happening, here and now. When we are breathing in, we can feel the cool air through our nostrils. When we are exhaling, we can feel the gentle constriction of our abdominal walls. If the wind through the trees outside our window creates a rustling sound, we notice it, and we hear it. We feel our feet on the floor, our seat in the chair, and our backs, straight and supported as we sit. Of course, even those of us who have practiced mindfulness for decades do not remain in direct, clear contact with the present moment all of the time. Rather than "staying present" in a fixed and rigid way, we might think of contact with the present moment as an act of returning, again and again, to what is happening here and now.

Contact with the present moment has value in that our lives are always lived, quite literally, *here and now*. By cultivating such contact, we are more open to our interaction with our environment, and we may more effectively shape our behavior toward intrinsically rewarding, valued directions. Beyond this, contact with the present moment may help to facilitate our experiencing thoughts *as* thoughts, emotions *as* emotions, and bodily sensations *as* bodily sensations. In this way, cognitive fusion, which often shows up as worry or as rumination, may be undermined. Anxiety disorders and depression are often characterized by anxious apprehension, worry, and rumination. Accordingly, if we can contact the present moment, and change the way in which we relate to these mental events, perhaps we can encounter some degree of freedom from unnecessary suffering. As we are less attached, fused, or identified with our worries of the future and ruminations upon the past, these mental events may exert less of a narrowing influence upon our range of behaviors, and we may be able to act more effectively across time and situations. Of course, each and every one of these situations will actually take place *here and now*.

In a clinical application, an ACT therapist may begin to train contact with the present moment using a simple exercise in practicing mindfulness of the breath. Such an exercise doesn't need to be an elaborate meditation technique. It also might only take a few minutes, at first.

Here is an example of an introductory exercise in contact with the present moment that might be used in an ACT-consistent way. In session, the therapist would ask the client's permission to engage in an experiential exercise, with eyes closed, which would introduce the experience of contact with the present moment. Clients would then be invited to place their feet on the floor, feel their body supported in their chair, and to feel their back, aligned as straight as possible. Clients would then be asked to close their eyes. The therapist would then guide clients to pay attention to the physical sensations that present themselves as they breathe in, and breathe out. The therapist might suggest that clients notice the gentle rising and falling of the abdomen and ribs as the breath moves in and out of the body, at its own rhythm and its own pace. Clients would be guided to merely observe, and make space for, any thoughts, feelings or images as they emerge in awareness. Whenever such thoughts might arise, they may be met with acceptance and curiosity, as clients gently draw their attention back to the flow of the breath. Such an exercise might continue for 3 minutes or so at first.

If this exercise sounds very familiar, there is a good reason. Essentially, training in contact with the present moment is training in mindfulness. Mindfulness exercises such as the body scan or mindfulness of the breath (Kabat-Zinn, 1990) are, in fact, excellent training vehicles for cultivating an ongoing, growing capacity for contact with the present moment. In addition to these seated or reclining clinical meditation methods, applied mindfulness exercises like mindfulness of walking or mindfulness of cooking can help to foster a generalized application of contact with the present moment.

Although contact with the present moment does have a direct and clear relationship with mindfulness, an ACT conceptualization of mindfulness does not rest in this contact with the present alone. As we have noted, there are three other core hexaflex processes that also involve elements of mindfulness, these being acceptance, self as context, and defusion.

DEFUSION

Defusion, the second ACT process we will discuss, is a new word that has been invented by the RFT community, just as so many psychological terms have been created over the years to explain new perspectives on human behavior. It represents the opposite of "cognitive fusion," which we discussed earlier. Accordingly, defusion basically means experiencing thoughts and feelings as what they really are (events in the mind), rather than what they say they are (events in the environment).

As we have seen, "cognitive fusion" represents our tendency to respond to thoughts and feelings as though they were literal events in the world. The term "fusion" also represents our tendency to allow our distressing, literalized mental events to exert direct control over our behavior. If I tell myself, "this is hopeless" and then avoid a job interview because I believe that there is no point in pursuing this aim, I can be described as being under the influence of cognitive fusion. We might imagine clients with terrible health anxiety, who fear that any human contact will lead to a virulent and deadly infection. These clients' fusion with thoughts about contamination might lead them to avoid human contact and deny themselves the opportunity for relationships, occupational advancement, or participation in their community. The impact of fusion with distressing thoughts, and ensuing experiential avoidance, can cause our behavioral options to narrow, and our lives to atrophy.

Traditional cognitive therapy techniques tend to challenge or dispute the logic, validity, or utility of disturbing thoughts through a process known as "cognitive re-structuring" (Beck et al., 1979). Cognitive defusion has a different purpose altogether. In cognitive defusion, the therapist does not aim to dispute a thought or directly change its content. Instead, the therapist attempts to alter the context in which clients experience the thought. By doing this, the therapist changes the relationship between the clients and their thoughts. As a result, clients are able to further open up their behavioral options, even in the presence of this disturbing thought. Cognitive content may change through defusion, particularly on the level of our thoughts about our thinking; however, this change in content is ancillary to the change in the function of mental events. As such, defusion represents our capacity to alter the distressing or unwanted functions of mental events without necessarily aiming to change their content, structure, or frequency (S. C. Hayes, Luoma, et al., 2006).

Over the years of ACT's development, many defusion techniques have been developed that often involve metaphors, perspective-taking shifts, and thought exercises. These techniques can be found in many sources, such as the books *Get Out of Your Mind and Into Your Life* (S. C. Hayes & Smith, 2005), *Acceptance and Commitment Therapy* (S. C. Hayes, Strosahl, & Wilson, 1999), and *Things Might Go Terribly Horribly Wrong* (Wilson & DuFrene, 2010). There are also many exercises and ideas available at the website for the Association for Contextual Behavioral Science (ACBS; http://www.contextualpsychology.org).

Below, we've included an example of a defusion exercise that we've found helpful in our clinical work. It is brief, straightforward and illustrates the "feel" of defusion work. The outline of the technique might be copied and given to clients so that they can remember how to use this exercise on their own. As a result, this example is written in a voice that speaks directly to the client.

Thanking the Mind

Let's take a moment to think about how our minds work. Our minds are evolutionarily designed to spot problems and to go about finding ways to fix them. If our ancestors had not developed keen ways to solve problems, we might not even be here today. We are truly lucky that we have evolved to possess minds that are complex problem-solving machines, which work using words. Happily, most of us don't need to be preoccupied with running from predators, or searching out our next meal. Unfortunately, our minds are "always on" and will try to generate thoughts to persistently solve problems, even when problems aren't there. Our minds generate frightening predictions about things that can happen in the future. Our minds generate images of the things that we regret from the past. Also, our minds are very good at creating and placing blame. Very often, we blame ourselves for things that are plainly not our fault. For a moment,

---

let's step back from this activity of our minds. What are our minds doing? Well, our minds are simply doing their jobs. Can we allow ourselves in this moment to actually thank our minds for trying to protect us, even though this protection sometimes provokes us to limit the possibilities in our life? If you will, imagine a recent situation that triggered your mind to generate a distressing thought. Recognize, in this very moment, that this thought, however upsetting it may be, is a product of your mind doing its job. Let's realize that we are not our thoughts and our thoughts are not reality. Probably for as long as we can remember, a stream of thoughts has been unfolding before our observing selves. For a moment, let's just thank our minds for trying to protect us. Let's recognize that we don't need to experience our thoughts as concrete, literal, or real. In doing so, perhaps we might choose to practice compassion in action that moves us forward in valued directions. Over the course of the next week, when you feel distress or tension, ask yourself "What is my mind telling me, right now?" See if you can make space for whatever is going through your mind in that moment, and even thank your mind for doing its job.

ACCEPTANCE

"Acceptance" in ACT represents our degree of willingness to remain in the presence of our experiences, with an open and receiving disposition, as we actively engage in the pursuit of our valued aims. In ACT, willingness is construed as an "alternative to experiential avoidance" (S. C. Hayes, Luoma, et al., 2006, p. 7). As we have noted, experiential avoidance is hypothesized to serve as a central process in the maintenance of psychological suffering. As you might expect, acceptance is obviously a very significant process in ACT.

In practicing acceptance, we are making space for the whole of our moment-by-moment experiencing. Even distressing or unpleasant thoughts, emotions and bodily sensations are consciously acknowledged, received, and allowed to move through the field of our awareness. Difficult experiences in life, whether internal experiences or events in the environment, can exert a degree of behavioral control over us, due to the nature of human verbal learning. This control can, of course, narrow our behavioral options. If we remember our earlier example of a terribly humiliating experience at a birthday party, we can imagine how people might try to avoid attending parties or drawing attention to themselves in public after such an experience. Experiential acceptance allows us to learn new behavioral options, even in the presence of mental events that tell us to flee, struggle, or hide. By ending our struggle to avoid our experiences, we might loosen the grip such experiences have upon us in the moment.

The word "acceptance" can sometimes connote endorsement or positive appreciation of an object. For example, I might "accept" a promotion at work or a gift from my friend. This makes sense, as the roots of the word "acceptance" come from a word meaning "to receive" or "to contain" (S. C. Hayes et al., 1999). In ACT we use acceptance in a different way. In speaking of acceptance, we aren't talking about giving up, giving in, or forcing ourselves to enjoy what we despise. For our purposes, acceptance means approaching life with open eyes and an open heart, and approaching our experience honestly, receptively, and realistically. This stance, in combination with defusion, contact with the present moment, and a transcendent sense of self, is fundamental to mindfulness from an ACT-consistent perspective.

Let's look at a clinical example of applied acceptance in action to help illustrate the potential value of cultivating willingness. Our client, Pete, is a 37-year-old attorney who has struggled with intense social anxiety since he was a teenager. He is prone to severe anxiety, and occasional panic attacks, when he enters group situations like dinner parties. As a result, he works very long hours and stays far clear of social situations. Even the thought of approaching a woman to make conversation, let alone ask her out for dinner, can cause paralyzing fear.

Pete's attempts to avoid anxiety through avoiding social situations have caused him to miss out on rewarding social interactions throughout his adult life. Beyond this, the more he has avoided these situations, and the harder he has tried to push away thoughts about his anxiety, the greater his fear has become. When he is forced into social situations through work or family obligations, he immediately becomes hypervigilant about a possible anxiety response. Pete checks in with his physical state repeatedly, and keeps asking himself if he can "handle it" or if he is "going to lose it." His persistent unwillingness to allow his experience to be what it is, moment by moment, has resulted in an intensification of anxiety, just as it has contributed to lost opportunities for meaningful experiences.

The following therapy vignette illustrates a segment of an ACT session that involves the therapist explaining the rationale for acceptance through the use of a metaphor. Metaphors are often used in ACT to help clients adopt a new perspective upon a habitual way of thinking, and to help foster a change in the way the clients relate to their mental events. After the use of the metaphor, the therapist walks through a form of applied acceptance known as "expansion" which is described by Russ Harris in his popular audience book, *The Happiness Trap* (Harris, 2007). ACT is based more upon processes than a cookbook approach to therapy techniques, so the style of therapy you see here may seem different from what is specifically outlined in *The Happiness Trap* (Harris, 2007) or other sources. This leaves room for therapists to respond flexibly, in the moment, to whatever might emerge in the consultation room.

Clinical Example

Pete: All of this talk about acceptance is starting to scare me. I mean, I entered psychotherapy so that I wouldn't feel anxious anymore, and so I could spend more time around people. I'm not so crazy about the idea of, you know, "feeling my feelings." The whole thing seems pretty nerve-wracking.

Therapist: Well that makes a lot of sense, actually. Based on what we've discussed, it sounds like you've been struggling with some pretty intense anxiety in social situations for a very long time. How many times would you say you've lost an opportunity to share the company of other people, because you were just too scared to face them?

Pete: Gosh, I can't even count that high. I suppose thousands and thousands of times.

Therapist: So it does seem that your efforts to stay away from anxiety actually have cost you quite a bit. In the ACT work we are doing together, I have no interest in you just "feeling your feelings" for the sake of feeling them.

Pete: I thought that was the point.

Therapist: Well, it is important to contact and be with our experiences, but not as an end in itself. My hope for you is that you can gain some freedom of action, in order to live the life you're hoping for. You've told me how much it would mean to you to build close relationships. I want to ask you a kind of tough, but important, question. If remaining in the presence of anxious thoughts and uncomfortable bodily sensations turned out to be a necessary part of you opening your life up to connection with other people, might you be willing to feel those feelings?

Pete: Yeah. At least, I believe so, but I'm just not sure how this is supposed to work. I mean, why does my avoidance create so much trouble for me? How does it make my anxiety worse?

Therapist: Let's imagine an action movie, like an old cliffhanger or an Indiana Jones episode. You know the scene where someone falls into quicksand? They inevitably struggle to get out. When they do, they push down with their limbs and concentrate all of their weight at one point in space. This resistance drags them down. Pretty soon, there are just a few bubbles on the sandy surface.

Pete: (laughing under his breath) So I guess I'm sunk! There's no way out. That can't be what you're saying.

Therapist: I don't think the situation needs to be that bleak. From what I've heard, the best thing to do when dealing with quicksand is to spread out and float as much as you can. By keeping still and stretching across the surface, you more evenly distribute your weight, and you might make it out after all.

Pete: So the more I struggle the worst things can get. You know, Doc, this does make some sense to me. I'm not dumb, and I get what you're trying to say. My question is, how am I supposed to make this happen? It's all well and good for me to just tell myself to be more accepting, but I just have no idea how to do that in real life.

Therapist: Luckily, we can learn to cultivate acceptance. It can take a little time, but it is possible. Let's try an exercise together now that might make this a little clearer and, perhaps, more real. Would that be all right?

Pete: Sure, that's what I'm here for.

Therapist: Good. I'm wondering, as we discuss your moving toward social situations, does even the thought of being around others stir anything up in you? For example, when we imagine what it would be like for you to move toward the situations that you've avoided, to strike up conversations and subject yourself to the evaluation of others, does it provoke any anxiety even here?

Pete: Yes, of course it does. I get very nervous just thinking about it. What am I supposed to do about that?

Therapist: Well, rather than moving away from this anxiety or trying to tamp it down, let's practice making space for your experience right here and right now. Could we begin this small exercise at this point?

Pete: Sure.

Therapist: (slowly, evenly and with presence) For just a little while, close your eyes and draw your attention to the flow of your breath in and out of your body. Bring part of your attention to whatever physical sensations present themselves to you right now. (pauses) Allow the spotlight of your awareness to move from the soles of your feet gradually up to the top of your head. If any physical sensations stand out in your awareness as uncomfortable, unpleasant or disturbing, just notice that. (pauses) As you exhale, consciously let go of any attempts to struggle against this experience. As you breathe in, breathe attention into the part of the body that presents you with discomfort or uneasiness. Allow yourself to get close to this experience. (pauses) As much as you can, allow a gentle, willing curiosity to be present. Next, as you observe the inflow of the breath bringing attention into the body, see if you can create space around this physical sensation. We aren't embracing the sensation, nor are we pushing it away. In this moment, we are just letting it be what it is. Nothing more, and nothing less. As you breathe out, know that you are breathing out, and creating ever more space around this experience. Finally, as much as you can, just allowing the sensation to be there. If you feel the need to alter or fight this experience, make space for that, too. (pauses) Take a few moments to stay with this exercise a bit longer, and then exhale and let go of the whole thing. When you are ready, open your eyes and we can discuss what you noticed.

Pete: (after a few moments of breathing quietly with his eyes closed, Pete opens his eyes and looks around the room) Well, that was, uh, different.

Therapist: What did you notice?

At this point in the session, the therapist and client would de-brief around this experience. An ACT-consistent approach to this discussion would involve less analysis and more reflection. Both the therapist and the client would be practicing willingness and mindful awareness together, as they discuss whatever observations might have presented themselves to the client. As these mindfulness-based processes interact, the client may experience a shift in sense of self, which is very important to ongoing ACT work. The emergent sense of self that is inherent in mindfulness-based training is known as "Self as Context" in ACT, and it is the final mindfulness-oriented hexaflex process that we will discuss.

SELF AS CONTEXT

When people ask us who we are, we might respond by telling some form of "life story" that we identify with. Responses like, "My name is Gregg, I'm from New Jersey, and I'm a plumber," make perfect sense. From an ACT perspective, this sense of self is known as the "conceptualized self." It's a sort of narrative that we tend to buy into about who we are. However, mindfulness practice can allow for an experience of a different sort of self. This self exists as a sort of observer, a silent "you" who has been watching your experience, moment by moment, for a very long time. This is sometimes referred to as "The Observing Self," or a "Transcendent Self," but is most often referred to in ACT as "Self as Context."

How is it that this "observer self," distinct from an experiencing self, arises? In order to understand this, let's turn again to ACT's roots in research on human language and cognition, RFT. Part of human relational responding involves our establishing verbally constructed relationships that involve perspective taking. The following are examples of a few of these derived relations: "I" as opposed to "You,"

"Here" as opposed to "There," and "Now" as opposed to "Then." Through these processes, part of our experience of being involves a sense of ourselves as a perspective before which the entirety of our experience unfolds throughout our whole lives. This sense of ourselves as an observer is referred to as "Self as Context" in ACT, because this experiential sense of self does, indeed, serve as the context within which our experiences are contained (S. C. Hayes et al., 1999). This sense of an "observing self" is important, because although this observer can notice the contents of consciousness, it is not those contents themselves. We have a thought, but we are more than that experience, just in the way that we have a big toe, but we are more than that big toe. Emotions don't feel themselves, thoughts don't observe themselves, and physical pain doesn't experience itself. Throughout our lives, we can notice the presence of an "observing self," which may be awareness itself, before which all of our experiences arise, exist, and disappear in time.

This sense of self as context is particularly important, because it can augment and blend with processes such as contact with the present moment, acceptance, and defusion, to afford a nonattached and dis-identified relationship to our experiences. Having identified particular valued directions, abiding in the space of self as context can allow us to willingly observe whatever arises in mind, as we deeply engage with those behaviors that matter to us, here and now.

Self as context is accessed in ACT through a variety of methods. Metaphors, such as the *chessboard metaphor* and *house metaphor* (S. C. Hayes et al., 1999; Luoma et al., 2007) are often used, and are widely available through the references cited or at the ACBS website. In the chessboard metaphor, the therapist asks the client to imagine a vast, expansive chessboard. Upon the board two teams of chess pieces are having a war. One team represents "negative" thoughts and feelings, while the other team represents "good" thoughts and feelings. Clients are asked where they are in this metaphor. What do they identify with in this chess game? Clients may respond in many ways. They may identify with the "good thoughts" or the "bad thoughts." After a brief discussion of this, the therapist can reveal that, in this metaphor, the client is represented by the board. This suggests that the client's self as context abides in the pure awareness that remains throughout the client's life. Just as the pieces wage their war upon the greater context of the chessboard, our thoughts, emotions, physical sensations, memories, and daydreams unfold moment-by-moment before an observing self, which is big enough to contain the totality of experience.

VALUES

The final two core processes worked with in ACT, values and committed action, are not known as mindfulness-based processes. That being noted, these processes do interact with mindfulness and acceptance to help clients move toward increasing psychological flexibility. We will be discussing these final processes in less detail here than we invested in the previous four mindfulness processes, given the mission of this book. However, these concepts are essential to employing ACT interventions, and should be explored fully in the process of learning ACT.

In ACT, values are verbally construed, freely chosen, and intrinsically rewarding patterns of deliberate behavior that persist over time and space (Wilson & DuFrene, 2008). These values are more like vectors or trajectories than they are goals or ends in themselves. Valuing is a quality that we can bring to all of our activities, to some degree. It reflects our capacity to bring intention and purpose to our actions, and the property of valuing is such that values authorship functions to establish patterns of reinforcement that can shape the path, tone, and tenor of our lives.

Rather than understanding values as secret, static dimensions in our lives, we can come to understand values as consistently evolving sets of behaviors and reinforcers. Because the reinforcement in valued activities emerges from the action itself, our values are bound to change, grow, and shift throughout our lives. For example, a very young boy may value putting on a toy cowboy hat and running through the woods with his friends with a cap gun. As he grows older he may sit with a similar dime-store Stetson hat and value plucking out the first few bars of a country and western tune on a cheap guitar before his grandfather's warm, appreciative eyes. During his teenage years, this same young man might feel thrilled to play a high school dance, strumming along to a current country hit, while his junior year crush stares back at him with flirtatious energy in the air. Later in life, this same person may sit beside the fire in his mid-70s, finger-picking Appalachian classics with a sense of mastery and accomplishment won through decades of dedication to his art and his passion. He may even take deep pride in passing along his craft to his own son or grandson. The value of connecting with the country and western music tradition has evolved and changed over time. Nonetheless, the pattern of instantiating this value has motivated, inspired, rewarded, and shaped this person throughout the course of his life. We can see in this example that the value is not an end in itself, but an ongoing dynamic pattern.

COMMITTED ACTION

In this last ACT core process, we find an emphasis on our taking committed, effective action to realize our values (S. C. Hayes, Luoma, et al., 2006). Direct behavior change methods, similar to those found in earlier forms of behavior therapy, may be applied in the service of a client's values. Some of these behavioral methods might include exposure to anxiety-provoking stimuli, assertiveness training, skills development, monitoring problematic behaviors, or pursuing abstinence from addictive behaviors.

In ACT, commitment isn't a one-time decision to pursue a value. In fact, the nature of being human means that we may need to renew our commitments and reinvest our energies in a dedicated pattern of action that serves our valued aims. Just as in 12-Step work, wherein people may undertake their commitment to sobriety "one day at a time," committed action in ACT involves choosing again and again to broaden our range of behavior, to remain in the presence of what we might not wish to face, and to persevere in the service of that which we have determined gives our lives value and meaning.

Such commitment may take place "one day at a time," and yet sometimes this choice to remain committed, this promise to oneself, might need to be made one moment at a time. It may be an act of compassionate returning to one's purpose, even amidst a sense of failure, humiliation, or shame. As a result, we can see how acceptance, defusion, self as context, contact with the present moment, and clear, enduring values may facilitate committed action as a gentle returning to a course we have feely chosen, even when we face pain, and wish to run from that pain in any way that we can devise.

SUMMARY

Among the field of mindfulness and acceptance-based cognitive and behavioral therapies, ACT is distinct on several levels. Rather than simply adding clinical meditation training to a set of therapy techniques, ACT research has operationalized and defined mindfulness at the level of basic behavioral processes. The processes which are described as comprising mindfulness include distinguishing a conceptualized self from a contextual self, contacting the present moment, expanding a sense of willingness, and practicing defusion from the literalized context of mental events. These processes have their foundation in an ongoing experimental research program into the nature of language and cognition, known as RFT. In turn, this account of language and cognition has its roots in a specific philosophy of science, being Functional Contextualism.

ACT is not designed to serve as a tool kit of therapy techniques used to target specific clusters of symptoms. Rather, in ACT we can find a mindfulness and acceptance-based process model of human psychological well-being. As the components of applied mindfulness are delineated in this approach, focused methods for cultivating applied mindfulness abound within ACT, including meditative exercises, metaphors, defusion techniques, and "eyes-open" experiential exercises. In this way, ACT invites clients to bring mindfulness directly into their day-to-day experiences.

The existing body of research evidence suggests that ACT is a clinically effective therapy modality, which works through processes that are different from traditional CBT and other treatment methods (S. C. Hayes, Luoma, et al., 2006; Forman et al., 2007). Component analyses and mediational analyses have suggested that the hexaflex processes discussed are, indeed, involved in mediating positive therapy outcomes (Bond & Bunce, 2000; Zettle & S. C. Hayes, 1987; S. C. Hayes, Luoma, et al., 2006). The controlled outcome study research in ACT is relatively young, and more research needs to be conducted to determine ACT's overall efficacy relative to other cognitive and behavioral treatments. Nonetheless, the research on ACT is encouraging. Accordingly, in ACT we can find a Western applied science of mindfulness and acceptance that is firmly rooted in a comprehensive approach to psychological research, from experimental research on basic cognition through randomized controlled outcome trials. ACT and RFT represent a thoroughly scientific and methodologically rigorous application of themes of willingness, presence, and mindful awareness that have their historical origins in ancient wisdom.

FOR MORE INFORMATION

Hayes, S. C., Stroshal, K. D., & Wilson, K. G. (1999). *Acceptance and Commitment Therapy: An Experiential Approach to Behavior Change.* New York: Guilford Press. This is the first major ACT book written by the founder. It contains a broad overview and specific examples.

Association for Contextual Behavioral Science (ACBS; http://contextualpsychology.org/). ACBS is an international society for ACT and RFT. It contains a wealth of information and resources.

Chapter 7

Other Mindfulness
Group Approaches

The success of MBSR and MBCT has stimulated a number of other group approaches that incorporate mindfulness for more diverse clients and presenting issues. Although mindfulness itself should not be considered a panacea, it appears to be a powerful tool that can serve as an important component for other therapeutic interventions.

In some cases, only minor modifications are likely to be necessary to adapt the already proven MBCT model to other presenting issues (such as anxiety rather than depression). However, some disorders and populations are likely to require significant changes to the standard 8-week model. Clinicians must be cautious when adapting new models. For example, a traditional MBCT group could worsen symptoms of posttraumatic stress, as the awareness fostered by mindfulness could amplify trauma-related anxiety symptoms in a setting that did not permit an individual to systematically process the trauma. Given the possibility of making clients worse, careful research and modification to the standard protocols are needed.

Likewise, certain populations are likely to require significantly different approaches. For example, children and individuals with profound developmental disabilities will require more concrete instructions and examples, as well as shorter mindfulness practice periods due to greater challenges in sustaining attention.

In this chapter, we will investigate mindfulness-based group interventions for chemical dependency, eating disorders, relationship enhancement, children and adolescents, parenting, geriatric populations, and inpatient populations. Preliminary research on these interventions appears very promising.

CHEMICAL DEPENDENCY

As those who have done work in the field know, chemical dependency counseling is very challenging work, with significantly high relapse and failure rates. Relapse prevention is much more challenging than initial abstinence from the substance. As Mark Twain said, "It's easy to quit smoking. I've done it hundreds of times." Of course, the problem with alcohol, tobacco, marijuana, and other drugs is that they actually do work to reduce anxiety, at least in the very short term, and hence are strong negative reinforcers. Mindfulness appears to help clients tolerate the negative affect associated with urges and withdrawal symptoms.

Alan Marlatt has made significant contributions to the field of psychological treatment of chemical dependency and relapse prevention (e.g., Marlatt & Gordon, 1985). In more recent years, he has incorporated mindfulness into his work (Witkiewitz & Marlatt, 2007; Witkiewitz, Walker, & Marlatt, 2005). Borrowing from the work of Kabat-Zinn (1990) and Segal et al. (2002), Marlatt, along with colleagues such as Sarah Bowen, has been instrumental in the development and study of Mindfulness-Based Relapse Prevention (MBRP) (Bowen, Chawla, & Marlatt, 2010).

MINDFULNESS-BASED RELAPSE PREVENTION

MBRP incorporates training in mindfulness as presented in MBSR and MBCT, as well as standard cognitive-behavioral therapy. However, it also includes several unique aspects, such as bringing mindfulness to urges, behavior chains, and relapse prevention.

Marlatt has long used the term "urge surfing" to refer to the ability to stay with the strong urges to use, and to "ride them," waiting for the urges to build, crest, and subside (Marlatt & Gordon, 1985). Mindfulness appears to enhance this ability – maintaining awareness of one's thoughts related to the urges, one's emotional state related to the urges, and the physical sensations that accompany the urges. By learning to be present and stay with the urges, the behavior of using can be decoupled from the thoughts, feelings, and sensations.

Another common strategy in chemical dependency work is tracing back the chain of events that led to a slip or relapse. For instance, a client may say that harsh words from a partner created so much anxiety that she had to take a drink. However, tracing back the situation may reveal that the client was feeling particularly lonely and vulnerable, and made choices that may have contributed to escalating an argument with the partner. Mindfulness can help a client to be more conscious of sensations, thoughts, and feelings moment to moment, so that adaptive behavioral choices can be made before such choices become too difficult.

Marlatt also talks about the "abstinence violation effect" (Marlatt & Gordon, 1985). Basically, once clients relapse, they are tempted to just give up and go back to regular use. MBRP incorporates the use of mindfulness in one's strategies to recover from slips to help clients continue to make progress toward recovery.

MBRP is delivered through eight sessions, and follows a format very similar to MBCT, which includes homework between sessions. MBRP incorporates a Rogerian, motivational interviewing (MI) style (Bowen, Chawla, & Marlatt, 2010; Marlatt, 2010). Indeed, Stephen Rollnick (2009), one of the pioneers of MI, states that mindfulness is quite compatible with a motivational interviewing style, which is commonly used in chemical dependency counseling. As with other mindfulness groups, though there is a manual for important techniques and topics to cover in each session, the practitioner is encouraged to be spontaneous and creative to adapt to the needs of a particular group (Bowen et al., 2010; Marlatt, 2010).

The theme of session one is "automatic pilot and craving." Introductions are made, rules for confidentiality are discussed, and the facilitator gives an overview of the course. Participants are introduced to mindfulness by eating a raisin, and by using the body scan. There is a discussion of how cravings work, and why people often succumb to them.

In session two, the focus is on triggers, thoughts, emotions, and cravings. The body scan is done again, and the previous week's homework is discussed. The cognitive-behavioral "ABC" model (Activating event, Belief, Consequence) is discussed, and how triggers can lead to relapse.

Bringing mindfulness into everyday life is the theme of session three. Participants are taught mindfulness of breathing, sights, and sounds. They are also taught the "three-minute breathing space" (as discussed in chapter four) and a walking meditation. A video featuring Jon Kabat-Zinn teaching an MBSR class is shown to highlight how mindfulness can be used for a variety of issues.

Session four teaches clients the importance of staying present and aware in high-risk situations. In addition to continuing to practice previous mindfulness techniques, participants are taught mindful stretching as another way of incorporating awareness into movement and everyday life. The facilitator brings up the topic of high-risk relapse situations, and asks participants to discuss personal scenarios that are likely to put them at risk for relapse.

Session five deals with finding a balance between acceptance and change. The mindfulness techniques are further refined, and the three-minute breathing space is taught as a means of finding some space to make good decisions when cravings or other triggers arise.

The sixth session focuses on thoughts, and how they can become triggers for relapse. Participants are taught more techniques for working with potentially distressing thoughts, and are taught that an occasional lapse does not have to lead to a full-blown relapse.

Session seven focuses on self-care. Participants are taught to notice how relapse can start long before the actual use of the substance occurs, and mindfulness can be used to bring awareness to these factors so as to help prevent use long before the substance is at hand. Participants create "coping cards" as tools to help remind them of ways to manage temptation.

The last session seeks to apply what has been learned for balanced living. Participants work on ways to develop their support networks and to reduce barriers that might prevent them from seeking help when needed. The entire course is reviewed, and plans are made for how to continue using mindfulness to deal with future challenges.

Because MBRP is relatively new, more research needs to be done to determine its effectiveness and to determine more precisely which aspects of the program are most important in achieving positive results. However, preliminary research, which includes randomized trials, looks very promising (Bowen, Chawla, Collins, Witkiewitz, Hsu, Grow, et al., 2009; Witkiewitz & Bowen, 2010; Witkiewitz & Marlatt, 2007; Witkiewitz, Walker, & Marlatt, 2005).

MBRP and Smoking Cessation

MBRP and mindfulness principles have also been applied to tobacco cessation. In our experience with chemical dependency work, clients have said that it is harder to quit smoking than it is to quit crack cocaine. Cigarettes are freely available everywhere, clients may have family members who continue to smoke around them, and actors are often portrayed smoking in film and television. This creates continual triggers for cravings. Also, the immediate physiological benefit of nicotine, with the immediate negative reinforcement of the reduction of anxiety, make the behavior of smoking one more cigarette difficult to stop when contrasted with the remote possibility of contracting lung cancer years down the road.

For her doctoral dissertation, Sarah Bowen (2008) and her chair Alan Marlatt studied the effects of mindfulness-based instructions on negative affect, urges, and smoking. This study introduced mindfulness-based training utilizing the urge-surfing technique to a group of undergraduate smokers. Interestingly, the experimental group and the control group did not differ significantly on measures of urges to smoke and negative affect. However, there was a stronger relationship between those urges and negative affect in the control group. That is, in the control group, negative affect was more likely to lead to stronger urges, and urges were more likely to lead to negative affect. Those using the mindful urge-surfing technique actually smoked fewer cigarettes in a 1-week followup, suggesting that they learned to experience the urges in a new way (Bowen & Marlatt, 2009).

EATING DISORDERS

Working with individuals with eating disorders can be very challenging and requires special training. The long-term mortality rate is over 10% for individuals with Anorexia Nervosa who have been hospitalized, most often because of heart failure due to electrolyte imbalances (American Psychiatric Association, 2000). Individuals with eating disorders often experience anxiety and low self-esteem, and have a skewed perception of their body proportions. Mindfulness can help with each of these challenges.

The original MBSR program of Jon Kabat-Zinn (Kabat-Zinn, 1990), and most other similar mindfulness-based groups, begins with a mindful eating exercise. Participants in our mindfulness groups, even when not specifically related to eating disorders, often describe the development of a new relationship with food. The raisin exercise teaches them to become aware of the taste and experience of eating, so they are less likely to shove food down without tasting it. This process of slowing down allows one to feel the signals of satiation. It also allows one to notice the difference between eating impulsively and eating when the body is hungry. By developing the ability to sit with uncomfortable emotions, watching them come and go, one is less likely to use food to avoid unpleasant emotional states.

MINDFULNESS-BASED EATING AWARENESS TRAINING (MB-EAT)

Although it is not the only intervention that incorporates mindfulness in the treatment of eating disorders, below is an outline of the MB-EAT model of Kristeller and colleagues (Kristeller, 2003; Kristeller, Baer, & Quillian-Wolever, 2006; Kristeller & Hallett, 1999). MB-EAT utilizes a comprehensive and systematic curriculum.

Outline of Sessions for MB-EAT Group

Session 1   Introduction to self-regulation model; Raisin exercise; Introduction to mindfulness meditation with practice in group. Assignment: Meditate with tape (continues all sessions).

Session 2   Brief meditation (continues all sessions); Mindful eating exercise (cheese and crackers); Concept of mindful eating; body scan. Assignment: Eat one snack or meal per day mindfully (continues all sessions with increasing number of meals/snacks).

Session 3   THEME: Binge triggers. Binge trigger meditation; Mindful eating exercise (sweet, high-fat food). Assignment: Mini-meditation before meals.

Session 4   THEME: Hunger cues – physiological vs. emotional. Hunger meditation; Eating exercise: Food choices – cookies vs. chips; healing self-touch. Assignment: Eat when physically hungry.

Session 5   THEME: Taste satiety cues – type and level of cues; Taste satiety meditation; Seated Yoga. Assignment: Attend to taste and satisfaction/enjoyment.

Session 6   THEME: Stomach satiety cues-type and level of cues. Satiety meditation; Pot luck meal. Assignment: Stop eating when moderately full; Eat at a buffet.

Session 7   THEME: Forgiveness. Forgiveness meditation. Assignment: Eat all meals and snacks mindfully.

Session 8	THEME: Inner wisdom. Wisdom meditation; Walking meditation. Assignment: Eat all meals and snacks mindfully.
Session 9	THEME: Have others noticed? Where do you go from here? Relapse prevention; Celebratory pot luck meal.
Follow-up Sessions	Meditation practice; Review of progress; Other weight management approaches. (Kristellar, Baer, & Quillian-Wolever, 2006, p. 81)

EMPOWER

Another 15-week mindfulness-based program undergoing research, called EMPOWER (Enhancing Mindfulness for the Prevention of Weight Regain), focuses specifically on weight loss maintenance; that is, on keeping a long-term healthy relationship with food. Wolever and Best (2009) describe the nine core skill sets that they believe are fundamental to recovery from eating disorders:

1. to nonjudgmentally observe the bundle of reactive thoughts, emotions, and body sensations that drive behavior;
2. to separate emotions from this bundle of reactivity;
   a. that emotions are transient events that often do not require response;
3. to separate thoughts from this bundle of reactivity;
   a. that thoughts are just thoughts, transient events that often do not require response;
4. to separate and tolerate behavioral urges from this bundle of reactivity;
5. to clarify physiological signals of hunger and fullness (gastric satiety);
6. to attend to taste-specific satiety;
7. to discern the physiological signature of appetite regulation cues (5 and 6) from emotions (e.g., the difference in anxiety and hunger; the difference in peaceful and stuffed);
8. to discern the true need underlying the reactivity; and
9. to make a wise and informed decision about addressing this true need. (Wolever & Best, 2009, p. 272)*

---

* From "Mindfulness-Based Approaches to Eating Disorders" by R. Q. Wolever and J. L. Best, in *Clinical Handbook of Mindfulness* [Edited by F. Didonna; p. 272], 2009, New York: Springer. Copyright © 2009 by Springer Science + Business Media B.V. Reprinted with kind permission from Springer Science + Business Media B.V.

MINDFULNESS FOR COUPLES

The relationship we have with an intimate partner is very special. Mindfulness principles are now being used for the enhancement of one of our greatest sources of connection and comfort.

J. W. Carson et al. (2004) published a study that showed promising results for a mindfulness-based relationship enhancement program on nondistressed couples. They reported improvements in day-to-day relationship happiness or satisfaction, reductions in levels of relationship stress, more effective stress coping, and reductions in overall levels of stress.

The Mindfulness-Based Relationship Enhancement (MBRE) program is a skills training group that was modeled after Kabat-Zinn's (1990) MBSR program, with accommodations to meet the needs of working in coupled dyads. These couple-specific adaptations include placing a greater focus on the partner for such meditation practices as loving-kindness. The model also incorporates partner versions of Yoga exercises, often using a partner for physical support. It also includes a mindful touch exercise, which involves receiving a gentle backrub, with a discussion of how mindful touch relates to sensual intimacy. Participants also engage in an activity where they are encouraged to gaze into each other's eyes and recognize the "deep-down goodness" in one another. Couples are encouraged to incorporate shared activities in their pleasant events calendar and to identify difficult communications or stressful interactions. A general session guide to the program is included below. Note the similarities to Kabat-Zinn's program, as well as the modifications made for couples.

Intervention Sessions for Mindfulness-Based Relationship Enhancement

Session 1 Introduction to program and mindfulness, loving-kindness meditation (focusing on partner), body scan. Homework: body scan, mindfulness of shared activity.

Session 2 Discussion of homework, body scan, sitting meditation – awareness of breath. Homework: body scan, use pleasant events calendar including shared activities.

Session 3	Discussion of homework, sitting meditation, individual Yoga. Homework: alternate body scan and Yoga plus meditation, use stressful communication calendar including communication with partner.
Session 4	Discussion of homework, sitting meditation, eye-gazing exercise and discussion. Homework: alternate body scan with Yoga plus meditation, use stressful communication calendar including communication with partner.
Session 5	Discussion of homework, sitting meditation, communication exercises. Homework: Alternate sitting meditation with Yoga, mindful attention to life impact on relationship, explore options for mindful responding to challenges.
Session 6	Discussion of homework, partner Yoga, sitting meditation. Homework: alternate sitting meditation with Yoga, attention to obstacles and aids to mindfulness.
Full Day Session	Multiple sitting and walking meditations, individual and partner Yoga, mindful movement and touch, group and partner discussion.
Session 7	Discussion of full-day session, sitting meditation, loving-kindness meditation, mindful touch. Homework: self-directed practice.
Session 8	Discussion/review of program, partner Yoga, sitting meditation, wrap-up.

(Adapted from J.W. Carson et al., 2004, p. 478)

Though initial results appear promising, more research is needed to refine the design of programs to enhance our intimate relationships.

MINDFUL PARENTING

Those of us who are parents know that it can be one of the most stressful and challenging, as well as the most pleasurable and rewarding, aspects of our lives. Parenting can give us an opportunity to continuously practice mindfulness, being present and engaging fully with our children. It is no surprise that mindfulness training is now being developed for parenting.

Myla and Jon Kabat-Zinn (1997) describe mindfulness and parenting in their book *Everyday Blessings: The Inner Work of Mindful Parenting*. They offer seven intentions for parents to work to build:

1. I will bring my entire creative genius to the work of mindful parenting.
2. I will see parenting as a spiritual discipline . . .
3. I will cultivate mindfulness and discernment in my daily life, especially with my children, using an awareness of my breathing to ground me in the present moment.
4. I will make every effort to see who my children actually are, and to remember to accept them for who they are at every age, rather than be blinded by my own expectations and fears. By making a commitment to live my own life fully and to work at seeing and accepting myself as I am, I will be better able to accord a similar acceptance to my children . . .
5. I will make every effort to see things from each child's point of view and understand what my child's needs are, and to meet them as best I can.
6. I will use whatever comes up in my own life and in the lives of my children, including the darkest and most difficult times, as "grist for the mill," to grow as a human being so that I am better able to understand my children, their soul needs, and what is required of me as a parent.
7. I will fold these intentions into my heart, and commit myself to putting them into practice as best I can, every day, and in appropriate ways that feel right to me and that honor my children's sovereignty, and my own. (M. Kabat-Zinn & J. Kabat-Zinn, 1997, pp. 382-383)

Mindfulness-Based Childbirth and Parenting (MBCP) was adapted from MBSR by Nancy Bardacke, RN, CNM, MA (Duncan & Bardacke, 2009). It is a 10-session program, meeting 3 hours once a week, with a 7-hour retreat between sessions 6 and 7. It is designed to teach mindfulness and coping skills to pregnant women and their partners or support persons. The classes also have a psychoeducational component, focusing on such things as the birthing process, breastfeeding, and the psychobiological needs of the infant. The classes also include a 15-minute snack break at the end to encourage socialization, because many new parents become socially isolated once their lives are consumed by a little one (Duncan & Bardacke, 2009).

Outline of Mindfulness-Based Childbirth and Parenting

Class One
History of MBCP/MBSR
Themes of the course
Definition of mindfulness
Raisin exercise

Class Two
Guided reflection, "Why are you here?"
Body scan
Working with painful sensations

Class Three
Physiology of childbirth and impact of stress
Process body scan homework
Sitting meditation
Adding mindfulness to daily activities

Class Four
Mindful Yoga
Using ice to practice working with pain
Bringing awareness to stressful experiences in daily life

Class Five
Using ice to practice working with pain
Education about birth process
Labor positions
Mindful touch to support partner

Class Six
Using ice to practice working with pain
Making wise choices for childbirth
Open awareness sitting meditation

Retreat Day
Body scan, mindful movement/Yoga, sitting meditation, and mindful eating
Introduction to walking meditation
Mindful speaking and listening practice

Class Seven
Introduction to loving-kindness meditation
Discussion of retreat day
Biological, emotional, and social needs of the newborn
Needs of the postpartum family

Class Eight
Mindfulness and breastfeeding
Postpartum depression

Class Nine
Alumni couple visits with their newborn to give their experiences
Course review
Graduation ceremony

Class Reunion
Meet newborns
Share stories

An initial pilot study of MBCP (Duncan & Bardacke, 2009) showed significant increases in mindfulness and positive affect, as well as lowered pregnancy anxiety, depression, and negative affect subsequent to taking the course. Participants also described qualitative benefits. Future research will need to incorporate randomized clinical trials.

CHILDREN AND ADOLESCENTS

There has not been much research to date on using mindfulness with children and adolescents. This is likely due to the fact that there is a great deal of variation in ability across developmental levels. Six-year-old children will process things much differently than 18-year-olds. Most research to date on mindfulness has focused on adults. Burke (2010) did a comprehensive analysis of the mindfulness literature on children and adolescents, and concluded that the current research shows support for the feasibility of mindfulness-based interventions (MBSR/MBCT models). However, much more empirical work needs to be done to develop a firm research evidence base.

Within the literature on mindfulness training for children, there has been some preliminary work suggesting unique modifications. Lee et al. (2008) published a study that discussed the acceptance and practicability of doing mindfulness-based groups with school-age children. Parents and children both endorsed receiving benefits from mindfulness-based training. The authors found that, with modifications, children were able to grasp the core concepts of mindfulness, were willing to engage in activities to learn mindfulness practice through a variety of sensory activities, and creatively found ways to extend what they learned into their daily activities. Complementary to this, Semple, Reid, and Miller (2005) published a study investigating the application of mindfulness-based treatment for children with anxiety, and found that mindfulness training can be an effective intervention. However, they caution that their study was limited and that further investigation of both the feasibility and efficacy of mindfulness training with children is needed. Napoli, Krech, and Holley (2005) looked at children with attention difficulties and found significant improvements in the ability for students who participated in mindfulness training to maintain attention as compared to students who did not. Their article provides activities that they used in their "Attention Academy" for teaching mindfulness skills.

In general, the consensus is that activities for teaching mindfulness to children will need to be kept shorter and more concrete, and should include a variety of sensory modalities for training. Clinicians such as Hooker and Fodor (2008) suggest that schools are ideal settings to introduce mindfulness to children. This may be because concepts such as "beginner's mind" are inherently a part of childhood. Children are developmentally in a state of learning and may not fall into the same traps that adults do with regard to being a "beginner." For children, their world is full of new experiences, whereas an adult may feel these are lessons already learned. The openness to experience that children often have is a wonderful starting point for teaching mindful habits. Furthermore, children attend school with the expectation that they will learn new things. This provides a primed setting for learning, and the use of mindful techniques may facilitate a productive start to the child's school day in homeroom. It can also be used for transitions in an effort to aid children in refocusing their attention throughout the day, bringing increased awareness to their school activities.

Saltzman and Goldin (2008) suggest that although the depth of mindfulness training for children comes from the clinician, it must be discussed in age-appropriate language and be fun and engaging. They further state that clinicians should not assume that their interpretation of words matches the child's understanding, and should seek to meet the children where they are. They offer an 8-session MBSR for Children course, and suggest that this can also be done in a child-parent setting. They provide child-oriented phrases for mindfulness concepts such as "funny mind" to describe negative internal dialogues that are often irrational or painful to experience. They explain exercises such as the "feelings practice," which includes artistic representations of the child's emotional experience, and the "Thought Parade," where children are taught to notice thought processes and to identify the intensity and strength of thoughts without judgment. Their program outcomes suggest that mindfulness can be a positive benefit to both children and adults.

Outline of 8-week MBSR for Children

Introduction to the Program
(Parents only): Introduce concepts of mindfulness, mindful eating (raisin exercise), review research/data on benefits of mindfulness, provide structure of program to parents.

Session 1
(Children or Children/Parents): Introduce concepts of mindfulness and a "Still Quiet Place," mindful eating, mindfulness of breath exercises, assign homework of daily practice and monitoring pleasant events.

Session 2
(Children or Children/Parents): Discussion about daily practice (formal and informal), mindful eating, Jewel/Treasure exercise, questions. Homework same as session 1, plus eating a snack or meal mindfully.

Session 3
(Children or Children/Parents): Continue formal/informal practice, observation of thoughts/feelings, attending to the body, mindful eating, introduce "funny mind," body scan. Homework body scan, monitor unpleasant events, notice stress, daily mindful activities.

Session 4
(Children or Children/Parents): Examine thoughts/feelings about unpleasant events, mindful eating, exercise on self/other perception, Yoga. Homework: body scan/Yoga, monitor unpleasant events, awareness of breath, daily mindful activities.

Session 5
(Children or Children/Parents): Discuss/deepen concept of "funny mind" and work to develop emotional fluency, mindful eating, explore thoughts/feelings, feelings practice. Homework: Feelings practice using art, poetry, and so on. Notice reactivity, begin a new daily mindfulness activity.

Vacation Week
Continue to practice without the support of class. Engage in mindful activities, notice reactivity.

Session 6
(Children or Children/Parents): Enhance capacity of observed thoughts/feelings through mindful eating, feelings practice with art/poetry, "Thought Parade" exercise, walking practice. Homework: "Thought Parade," take a "Thoreau Walk," feelings

	practice, difficult communication calendar, continue responding to stress and "funny mind."
Session 7	(Children or Children/Parents): Learn to apply mindfulness during difficult communication, begin loving-kindness practice, mindful eating, communication dyads (talking/listening exercise), role play ways of mindful responding. Homework: loving-kindness exercise, respond to stress and "funny mind," imagine world from someone else's point of view, bring something to share for the final class.
Session 8	(Children or Children/Parents): Develop ways to use mindfulness in the child's life, group choice mindful practice, write a letter to a friend, personalizing practice. Homework: Make a commitment to practice using your choice of exercises.

(Adapted from Saltzman & Goldin, 2008)

Mindfulness-Based Cognitive Therapy for Children (MBCT-C) is a 12-session group therapy for children ages 9 to 13 years old (Lee et al., 2008; Semple & Lee, 2011; Semple et al., 2010; Semple et al., 2005). MBCT-C is a developmentally appropriate adaptation of Mindfulness-Based Cognitive Therapy (Segal, Williams, & Teasdale, 2002). Semple and Lee (2011) have recently published a manual for treating children with anxious thoughts, and discuss theoretical change mechanisms in cognitive therapy and in mindfulness-based approaches, as well as how mindfulness can modify habits of anxious thinking. They describe the development and aims of MBCT-C, some of the adaptations made in working with children, and the 12-session program structure, and they review the research support for MBCT-C.

In general, there is promising data to suggest that children and adolescents can benefit from mindfulness training similarly to that of adults, and we believe that there will continue to be growth in this area. Further studies to support the use of developmentally appropriate adaptations for children will need to be done to have a more complete picture of how best to engage children in mindful practice and the benefits of such practice.

GERIATRIC
POPULATIONS

Lucia McBee (2008, 2009) is a pioneer in applying the principles of mindfulness with geriatric populations, using a model she calls Mindfulness-Based Elder Care (MBEC). McBee utilizes a CAM approach (Complementary and Alternative Medicine), which incorporates elements such as aromatherapy and gentle hand massage.

McBee has done much of her work in nursing homes, where the clients are no longer able to live independently. Because attention and memory can be particularly challenging with this population, significant modifications needed to be made to the MBSR curriculum.

Clients with moderate, and even severe, dementia still appear to benefit from mindfulness groups. Even with language and cognitive impairments, patients often respond positively to nonverbal cues, aromatherapy, and gentle touch. They appear to enjoy a peaceful, relaxing environment, and seem to resonate with the calm presence and tone of the therapist. For very impaired patients, the tone of the therapist's words is more important than the content. This highlights the importance of the therapist's own regular mindfulness practice (McBee, 2008).

Gentle Yoga, or stretching exercises, is also useful as a medium to teach mindfulness, especially for a population who may have restricted physical activity. Even individuals with cognitive impairments are often able to mimic movements patiently demonstrated by the therapist.

Because of the nature of scheduling in a nursing home, and because of challenges for patients to maintain attention due to physical and cognitive impairments, McBee (2008) restricts her sessions to 45 to 60 minutes. Also, due to the challenges of maintaining regular attendance, McBee uses an ongoing group format, with a different skill practiced each time.

Mindfulness-Based Elder Care Outline

- Group is started with a guided sitting practice, focusing on breath or body
- Participants check in about applying practice outside the group

---

- Introduction of a new exercise
  (eating mindfully, meditation on the breath, deep breathing, light stretching, guided imagery, body scan, standing and walking meditations)
- Process/discussion of new exercise
- Finish with silent meditation or visualization exercise

(McBee, 2008)

Although McBee asks patients to try to practice between sessions, she finds that many forget, or are unable to effectively use technology to play the CDs.

As McBee notes, well-controlled research with the geriatric population can be challenging, but an initial study of MBEC looks promising (McBee, Westreich, & Likourezos, 2004).

Being a caregiver of frail elderly individuals can sometimes be quite stressful, particularly if the individual is suffering from dementia. McBee (2008) has also adapted the MBSR program for use with caregivers, both personal caregivers and health professionals, to help reduce stress and prevent burnout.

For professional caregivers, such as those working in a nursing home, McBee (2008) made modifications to the MBSR program to fit the needs of the participants. Sessions are kept short (45-60 minutes) to minimize disruption of staffing. Participants are given journals, CDs, handouts, and homework assignments. Sessions begin with guided or silent mindfulness practice, gradually increasing the length of the meditation sessions over the length of the course. The focus is on both personal self-care and using mindfulness with patients. Topics for the sessions include discussions of what mindfulness is, mindfulness exercises, aromatherapy, light stretching exercises, visualization exercises, communication skills, hand massage, and palliative care. McBee (2008) reports that the initial qualitative findings of this group were very positive, and staff retention was increased.

INPATIENT SETTINGS

An acute psychiatric inpatient setting can at times feel chaotic. Patients come in with acute distress and are surrounded by others in distress. Mindfulness is a skill that can be helpful to cope with the chaos, and is something patients can take home with them after they leave the hospital.

The Department of Psychiatry of the Villa Margherita clinic in Vicenza, Italy has modified MBCT into a program called M-BPIT (mindfulness-based program in inpatient treatment) (Didonna, 2009b). The program was designed mainly for patients with mood disorders, anxiety disorders, and borderline personality disorder, who have a 4-week inpatient stay. The groups meet twice per week, 90 to 120 minutes per session. There are also two daily practice sessions, in the morning and evening, lasting 30 minutes each. Because of patient turnover, a similar format is used for each session, with exercises and themes rotating (Didonna, 2009b).

Mindfulness-Based Therapy Program in Inpatient Treatment

- After patients have settled down in the room on their mats or chairs and after the roll call (only the patients considered ready for treatment by the team of professionals are admitted to the session), the instructor starts to explain and illustrate the aims of the group, the general meaning and rationale of mindfulness for the patients' problems (problem formulation, acceptance, nonjudgmental attitude, exposure), and the consistence and integration of the group with the other therapies in the treatment program.
- Explanation of the first mindfulness exercise, normally chosen depending on the group composition of the given session, evaluating the possible problems of the patients present.
- Formal mindfulness exercise (20-40 min).
- Practice review and sharing comments on the exercise.
- Understanding the meaning and rationale of the exercise for the patients' problems using comments, suggestions, questions, difficulties and benefits that arose during the exercise.
- Break (10 min).
- Final meditation (10-15 min).
- Sharing comments on the exercise.
- Homework and handing out of material for participants (sheets, descriptions of exercises, quotations, CD for practice).

(From *Clinical Handbook of Mindfulness* [Edited by F. Didonna; p. 456], 2009, New York: Springer. Copyright © 2009 by Springer Science + Business Media B.V. Reprinted with kind permission from Springer Science + Business Media B.V.)

Didonna (2009b) provides more details about these inpatient groups, such as the types of obstacles and difficulties in inpatient groups, coping strategies to deal with difficulties, and exclusion criteria.

Although there are some studies demonstrating that mindfulness and acceptance-based therapies can be helpful in an inpatient setting (e.g., Bach & S. C. Hayes, 2002; Bohus et al., 2000; Gaudiano & Herbert, 2006; York, 2007), more research is needed.

FOR MORE INFORMATION

Mindfulness-Based Relapse Prevention
Bowen, S., Chawla, N., & Marlatt, G. A. (2010). *Mindfulness-Based Relapse Prevention for Addictive Behaviors: A Clinician's Guide.* New York: Guilford Press. A full-length book covering MBRP for use with addictions.

Mindfulness-Based Eating Awareness Training
Kristeller, J. L., Baer, R. A., & Quillian-Wolever, R. W. (2006). Mindfulness-based approaches to eating disorders. In R. A. Baer (Ed.), *Mindfulness and Acceptance-Based Interventions: Conceptualization, Application, and Empirical Support* (pp. 75-91). San Diego, CA: Elsevier. A clearly written chapter on using the MB-EAT intervention.

Mindfulness-Based Relationship Enhancement
Carson, J. W., Carson, K. M., Gil, K. M., & Baucom, D. H. (2004). Mindfulness-based relationship enhancement. *Behavior Therapy, 35*, 471-494. This journal article describes the MBRE program.

Mindfulness-Based Childbirth and Parenting
Duncan, L. G., & Bardacke, N. (2010). Mindfulness-based childbirth and parenting education: Promoting family mindfulness during the perinatal period. *Journal of Child & Family Studies, 19*, 190-202. doi 10.1007/s10826-009-9313-7. This journal article contains a full description of MBCP and results of the initial pilot study.

Mindfulness-Based Cognitive Therapy for Children
Semple, R. J., & Lee, J. (2011). *Mindfulness-Based Cognitive Therapy for Anxious Children: A Manual for Treating*

  Childhood Anxiety. Oakland, CA: New Harbinger. A full
  book providing details on using the MBCT-C intervention.

Mindfulness-Based Elder Care

  McBee, L. (2008). *Mindfulness-Based Elder Care: A CAM
  Model for Frail Elders and Their Caregivers.* New York:
  Springer Publishing. A full-length book devoted to using
  mindfulness with the geriatric population.

Mindfulness-Based Therapy Program in Inpatient Treatment

  Didonna, F. (2009). Mindfulness-based interventions in an
  inpatient setting. In F. Didonna (Ed.), *Clinical Handbook
  of Mindfulness* (pp. 447-461). New York: Springer. This
  book chapter goes into detail about the M-BPIT program.

Chapter 8

Individual Approaches to Using Mindfulness

With the notable exception of ACT (covered in Chapter 6), most of the empirical research on mindfulness has been focused on group interventions. One reason for this is because Kabat-Zinn (1990) first developed MBSR in a group hospital setting and designed his approach to teach skills rather than to provide psychotherapy. From an empirical standpoint, it is much easier to measure a time-limited group intervention than to attempt to measure how mindfulness can be applied to individuals. In the real world of clinical intervention, clients never present with one simple issue or diagnosis; mindfulness (or any other intervention) must be adapted to the unique characteristics and circumstances of each client.

Clinical experience and research to date also suggest that teaching mindfulness skills per se may best be done in a group setting, so that members can share their experiences and provide support to each other. However, arranging groups may be logistically challenging, and sometimes adaptations need to be made to work with individual clients.

As with Acceptance and Commitment Therapy and Dialectical Behavior Therapy, mindfulness will be best utilized as part of a comprehensive theory, and will be part of an intervention that effectively utilizes the most efficacious, proven techniques. We advocate incorporation of mindfulness into all of psychotherapy, or into an integrated system – we don't need yet another therapy in the collection of 800 or so that already exist.

Individual approaches to DBT and ACT were discussed in previous chapters. Here we will look at other approaches which are currently being investigated.

MINDFULNESS-BASED COGNITIVE THERAPY

Mindfulness-Based Cognitive Therapy has proven useful for the prevention of depressive relapse. However, clinicians in private practice may be unable to form groups with the frequency needed by clients, and may need to teach the material on an individual basis.

Zindel Segal (2008) reports that he spends the first part of a session practicing mindfulness with clients, then spends the second half doing the therapy work. Starting with mindfulness, as in the groups, sets the tone for the session, helping clients de-center from their thoughts and worries. If the client is restricted to 1-hour sessions, and half of the session is used for individual therapy work, it will of course take much longer than 8 weeks to get through the material. However, if the client commits to doing homework, the essence of the practice can be quickly experienced, and the principles can be incorporated into the specific therapeutic interventions.

OPEN MIND TRAINING

Ron Alexander (2008) utilizes a mindfulness-based approach called "Open Mind Training." Alexander's approach seeks to foster an open, creative mind through the development of "mindstrength," which he defines as "the ability to very quickly and easily shift out of reactive mode and become fully present in the moment, experiencing the full force of your emotions even as you recognize that they are temporary and will soon dissipate" (Alexander, 2008, p. 22).

Alexander's approach involves a three-step process: (a) letting go of resistance; (b) tuning in to your creative unconscious, experiencing open mind; and (c) moving forward with a practical plan for transformation.

Letting go of resistance involves acknowledging and working through obstacles, both inner and outer, that are keeping you from tuning in to yourself or accomplishing your goals. Tuning in to your creative unconscious involves listening to a deeper part of yourself, beyond the conventional, constricted sense of self, and allowing a sense of spacious, open mind to develop.

Moving forward with a practical plan involves making concrete goals and workable plans for achieving them. It also involves the inspiration of what Alexander calls a "wisdom council of support," that is, a group of wise and trusted friends and allies to help you maintain your vision and achieve your goals.

As an example of his training process, Alexander (2008) gives clients a five-step formula for discarding unwholesome self-judgments as part of the first step of letting go of resistance. First, the client is asked to notice and name any judgment that arises, such as "worthless." Next, the quality is investigated, in which related feelings that arise with the identified label are explored. Reminiscent of cognitive-behavioral therapy, the client is then asked to find a thought or feeling that could create a shift out of the particular feeling state. The client then holds the new thought and feeling as firmly as possible. Finally, the client assesses whether or not a shift has occurred, and if not, the above steps are repeated.

There has not yet been any controlled research on open mind training, though many of its tenets are based on established principles of mindfulness.

MINDFUL RECOVERY

Thomas and Beverly Bien (2002) have written a book for lay audiences called *Mindful Recovery*. They utilize a spiritual approach, in the sense of searching for greater meaning in one's life. The premise is that having meaning will help prevent relapse, and hence the focus is on the "maintenance" stage in Prochaska and DiClemente's (1992) stages of change model.

Often, individuals who have become addicted to substances have difficulty managing emotions, or feel overwhelmed by them. Mindfulness can help clients to stay in the emotion and to ride the waves of urges and other unpleasant feelings. It can also help clients to see the magic in everyday moments, in the feeling of the wind moving across the skin, or in the taste of a raisin, because daily life becomes bland after the intense rush of most substances (T. Bien & B. Bien, 2002).

Too often, we have seen individuals in self-help groups spend too much time thinking about not using. It is certainly laudable that these individuals want to stay clean, but they put themselves in a double-bind situation, where they spend a lot of time thinking about not doing something they crave doing. If you are asked not to think about a green elephant, it is impossible to remember not to think about a green elephant without thinking about a green elephant.

Although of course it is important to think about how one is going to avoid using substances, it is also crucial to have a bigger goal to move toward, a sense of spirituality or meaning about where one fits in the grand scheme of things. As Nietzche said, "[a person] who has a why can live with almost any how."

The Ten Doorways to Mindful Recovery

1. *Seeing the magic of the ordinary*
   Return to the present moment.
2. *Telling life stories*
   Consider your life as a story you are still writing.
3. *Journaling*
   Use journaling to deepen awareness of your life story and open the door to spiritual awakening.
4. *Meditating*
   Practice meditation to become more accepting of yourself and your life.
5. *Recreation and nature*
   Find ways to connect with the natural world.
6. *Loving*
   Cultivate healthy relationships to discourage addiction.
7. *Dreaming*
   Explore dreams to expand your view of who you are beyond the limited point of view of your conscious, rational self.
8. *Working*
   Practice mindfulness at work.
9. *Transforming negative emotions*
   Learn to hold and embrace difficult emotions to ensure successful recovery.
10. *Living moment by moment*
    Practice, practice, practice.

EATING
MINDFULLY

Many individuals in our modern culture struggle with maintaining a healthy weight and healthy eating habits. There is a love of food high in fat and processed sugar, and modern conveniences have reduced the activity levels of many children and adults. A study published in the *Journal of the American Medical Association* (Ogden et al., 2006) revealed that almost one out of five children are overweight, and almost one third of all adults are obese in the United States.

Given that there is also significant societal pressures to be thin, as is frequently portrayed in the media, it is no wonder that so many of us develop a love-hate relationship with food. Dieting fads are common, pulling for an "easy fix" for a lifetime of poor eating habits. Unfortunately, diets often fail because they create anxiety around eating and weight, and so often result in weight rebound.

Susan Albers (2003, 2006, 2008, 2009) has written extensively on the process of bringing mindfulness to eating. She takes a broad and comprehensive approach built upon building awareness and developing a balanced relationship with food. In her workbook *Eat, Drink, and Be Mindful*, Susan Albers (2008) outlines eight main principles for mindful eating. She first encourages clients to simply become more aware of their eating habits and not to try to change anything. Second, clients are taught to attend to their bodies, noticing such things as bodily signals of hunger. Third, clients are encouraged to make conscious decisions to eat, rather than simply engaging in automatic patterns. Fourth, clients are reminded to pay attention to environmental cues, noticing how eating habits change in different locations, and to not keep unhealthy foods in a visible place. Fifth, clients are encouraged to be present when eating, and not to do other things such as watching television. Sixth, clients can notice when judgments arise, such as those sparked by unreasonable societal pressures, and practice disengaging from them. Seventh, clients are taught to let go of expectations, so they can respond consciously to food cravings rather than react habitually. The eighth principle is to practice acceptance, to feel more comfortable with oneself and one's body as it is, and to avoid getting caught up in fad diets and ruminations.

COMPASSION FOCUSED THERAPY

As this book demonstrates, there are many, diverse mindfulness-informed psychotherapies. However, some psychotherapy innovators have looked beyond mindfulness to build new forms of therapy that involve other essential elements of Buddhist thought. For example, British psychologist Paul Gilbert (2005) has adapted evolutionary psychology, the neuroscience of emotion, and Buddhist methods for training in self-compassion, to develop a new variation on CBT known as Compassion Focused Therapy (CFT).

CFT is characterized by an emphasis on the client's specific "compassionate mind training." The rationale for CFT suggests that experiencing compassion actually represents a central process in emotion regulation. Compassionate mind training may be particularly useful when dealing with clients who struggle with feelings of shame and who exhibit self-critical thinking (Gilbert & Irons, 2005).

Dr. Gilbert (2007) describes compassion as a "multifaceted process" that has evolved from "the caregiver mentality" found in human parental care and child rearing. So, we can see that compassion involves a number of emotional, cognitive and motivational elements. These elements include care for the welfare of others, sympathy, distress-tolerance, empathy, nonjudgmental awareness, distress sensitivity, and the ability to create opportunities for growth and change with warmth (Gilbert, 2007). Gilbert (2009) defines compassion as a "basic kindness, with a deep awareness of the suffering of oneself and of other living things, coupled with the wish and effort to relieve it" (p. xiii).

The CFT model describes three primary emotion-regulation systems that we humans have developed through evolution (Gilbert, 2009). As we take this brief look at CFT, it is worth exploring a bit more about each of these systems (see Figure 2, p. 133)

The first of the three emotion-regulation systems is referred to as the "achieving and activating system" (Gilbert, 2007, 2009). This system involves the range of human behaviors that contribute to pursuing aims and seeking out the things that we either need, or that bring us pleasure. If you imagine the feeling that you might have if you just discovered that you've won a lottery that will pay off your mortgage, you can capture a taste of the activation of this incentive-focused system.

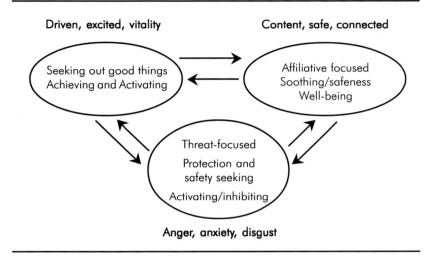

Figure 2. Types of Affect Regulation Systems
(Adapted from *The Compassionate Mind* by P. Gilbert, 2009, p. 22, London: Constable.
Copyright © 2009 by Paul Gilbert. Reprinted with permission from Constable Robinson.)

The second emotion-regulation system, known as the "threat/ protection system," involves a highly sensitive "threat focus" and involves what we have come to know as the "fight or flight" response, which really shows up clearly in the brain's limbic system and brainstem. Faced with persistent threats, such as predators, disease, and natural disasters, it seems that our ancestors evolved with a system for quickly detecting danger in the environment and responding rapidly.

In contrast, the third emotion-regulation system discussed in CFT is referred to as an affiliation oriented "soothing system." It is reflected in "affiliative-focused" behaviors, such as nurturance, validation, and empathy, all of which can involve the oxytocin and opiate systems (Gilbert, 2007). Humans have evolved to respond to kindness and warmth through a decrease in our anxiety systems and a felt sense of "soothing." This involves an evolved capacity for we humans to feel "safeness" and to feel soothed in the presence of stable, warm, empathic interactions with others (Gilbert, 2009).

One of the aims of CFT is training clients in accessing and employing this system of self-soothing through the felt experience of compassion. In CFT, therapists emphasize that every one of us has emerged from the flow of life, and the path of evolution, on this planet.

We did not choose to be here, nor did we choose our learning history, and the many difficult lessons that life can impart. We have a very tricky brain, with lots of challenging inborn capacities for cruelty, anxiety, and sadness. Our lives are very hard, and very short compared to the life of our planet or the stars. Suffering is a fundamental truth.

CFT aims to help patients to recognize all of this, and to recognize that, in a very real sense, all of this is not their fault. Beginning from a perspective of radical acceptance and self-forgiveness, CFT outlines a specific plan for training our compassionate minds. Such training involves mindfulness meditation, visualization exercises, and a series of cognitive and behavioral techniques, all of which are designed to help clients develop a stronger and more resilient capacity for self-compassion. Early outcome research and brain-imaging research from the CFT community is promising and may lead to more effective ways of addressing several psychological problems, such as anxiety, problematic anger, and shame-based difficulties in depression.

MINDFULNESS IN INTIMACY AND SEX

Our intimate relationships are very important to us. Given the usefulness of mindfulness in other areas of our lives, researchers are beginning to investigate the effects of mindfulness on relationship satisfaction. Mindfulness may also enhance sexual intimacy, and can be used in conjunction with traditional sex therapy techniques such as sensate focus.

Mindfulness and Relationship Satisfaction

Burpee and Langer (2005) investigated the role of mindfulness and perceived spousal similarity in level of marital satisfaction. Using a mindfulness scale developed by Langer to measure levels of novelty seeking, novelty producing, flexibility, and engagement, results showed a strong relationship between these scores and marital satisfaction. They concluded that partners who are mentally engaged and open to new experiences enjoy more satisfying relationships. They highlight that in a mindful state, couples are more ready to accept the changing nature of the relationship over time, and are more excited and malleable within that context. Additionally, the attitudes of nonjudgment that occur with mindfulness are suggested to be a potential factor in being more accepting of a partner.

Barnes et al. (2007) and Wachs and Cordova (2007) investigated the link between mindfulness in intimate relationships and relationship satisfaction. They collectively showed positive results for the role that mindfulness plays in positive feelings in couple relationships. They suggest that this is due to increased awareness, capacity for empathy, and improved communications seen in mindfulness practice. Mindfulness also appears to decrease the impulsive and hostile interactions that are often associated with relationship dissatisfaction.

Mindfulness and Sex

Brotto and colleagues (Brotto, Basson, & Luria, 2008; Brotto & Heiman, 2007; Brotto, Heiman, et al., 2008; Brotto, Krychman, & Jacobson, 2008) incorporate mindfulness into a psychoeducational treatment program for women with sexual desire and arousal disorders. They suggest that the addition of mindfulness-based training in nonsexual activity leads to greater awareness in sexual activities, and helps lead to an enhanced sexual arousal response in women. They use a combination of in-session activities and homework exercises with cognitive-behavioral therapy and traditional sex therapy activities. Participating women qualitatively reported that the mindfulness component was the most valuable aspect of treatment (Brotto & Heiman, 2007).

Brotto, Krychman, and Jacobson (2008) give examples of how mindfulness is incorporated into the treatment of sexual desire and arousal disorders. Women are initially taught to utilize the body scan activity illustrated by Kabat-Zinn (1990), as well as to incorporate informal mindfulness practice during other activities in their day. With the same attitude of mindfulness and nonjudgment, women are instructed to use a set of body-focused mindfulness exercises to practice at home. These exercises are borrowed from the masturbation program outlined in *Becoming Orgasmic* (Heiman & LoPiccolo, 1987). The authors use three 20-minute exercises.

The first exercise is simply called a "focusing exercise," in which participants are asked to visually attend to their bodies during and after a bath or shower. The women are encouraged to describe what they see in nonjudgmental ways. They are also given a list of possible statements to repeat to themselves during the exercise, such as, "My body is my own," "It is alive," and "I appreciate the following aspects of my body."

The second activity used is a "self-observation" exercise, which asks women to use a hand-held mirror to observe their genitals. The participants are provided an anatomical diagram of the female genitals, aimed to teach them to objectively label the different parts. This activity is done as a nonsexual exercise, with the only goal being to allow the women to remain present focused while letting any judgments about themselves, their bodies, or how they are struggling with the exercise to pass.

The third exercise is entitled "Self-Observation and Touch," and asks women to gently touch their genitals while repeating the self-observation exercise they practiced before. This practice is also identified as a nonsexual exercise, and is focused once again on nonjudgmental present awareness. After 6 weeks of practicing these three exercises, participants are asked to modify the activities to incorporate a sexual goal. The authors hypothesize that by increasing awareness, women will have greater arousal and satisfaction during sexual activities. They caution that this hypothesis needs further testing, providing an avenue for future directions in the use of mindfulness.

Honarparvaran et al. (2010) investigated the use of Acceptance and Commitment Therapy (ACT) in reducing sexual dissatisfaction among Iranian couples. Their results suggest that ACT has a positive effect on sexual satisfaction among couples, with these results being most pronounced for the male participants in their group.

We believe that the recent interest in applying mindfulness to the enhancement of couple relationships and sexual intimacy is an area that is open to future growth. Although the practice of mindfulness is primarily individually growth promoting, the benefits seen can be directly applied in interpersonal relationships and romantic partnerships. Continued investigation in this area will be necessary.

CASE EXAMPLES OF ADAPTING MINDFULNESS FOR INDIVIDUAL CLIENTS

The following case studies provide examples of some of the ways that mindfulness can be used with individual clients. Note that often the concepts are worked with directly, and are not even necessarily labeled as mindfulness. Often, the principles and the lived experience can be appreciated by clients, even if they are not interested in formal mindfulness training.

CASE EXAMPLE: "PANIC ATTACKS"

A client once came to me (RWS) with complaints of panic attacks. Immediately upon entering my office he appeared to be experiencing a great deal of anxiety, and placed his hand on his stomach with a look of nausea on its face. I immediately asked if he'd like to have a trash can next to him, which slightly decreased his anxiety. (Incidentally, he reported that he had not thrown up in over 4 years, but always felt like he would. He could not get rid of the thought that he was going to throw up, and that he should never eat very much food, and that he needed to avoid being around other people and going out socially for dinners.)

Because this client was experiencing panic right at that moment in the office, I used it as an opportunity to introduce the concept of mindfulness. However, there was no need to make mindfulness a thing, or a technique, or a theory. I simply asked him to narrate what was happening. By describing what is happening, the client begins to feel separate from the process. Typically, our thoughts and fears and worries become identified with our sense of who we are. By describing them, we are subtly reinforcing the fact that we are not our thoughts, feelings, or worries.

I asked him to begin by noticing his breathing rate. His breathing was perhaps 30 or 40 breaths a minute, which is double the normal breathing rate. Simply by calling attention to the process of breathing, which is both conscious and unconscious, he could exercise his conscious choice to slow down the breathing, which has a physiological effect. As he did this, I described for him the relationship between breathing, heart rate, and feelings of anxiety. Initially, he had difficulty slowing his breath, for he had developed a skewed idea of what normal breathing was. I made the suggestion that he count to eight as he inhaled and eight as he exhaled, and to breathe more deeply from the diaphragm rather than from the muscles of the chest. Though he still had some difficulty with the breathing, it did slow down somewhat.

I next asked him to describe other physical sensations he was having. When he said, "I feel like I'm going to die," I gently noted that that was a thought, and that we would look at the thoughts later, but asked him again to simply describe the physical sensations themselves. He described the sensation of his heart beating quickly, and he described a tingling sensation in his fingertips and in his lower legs. I asked him to simply watch those feelings.

Next, I asked him to describe the thoughts that were going through his mind. When he said, "I feel like I'm going to die," I asked him if he had had that thought before, and he said that he had, many, many times. I asked him to try to watch that thought as if he could say to himself, "Oh, there's that thought again. That's not who I am, but that's the thought I'm having again in this moment."

As he calmed down, I briefly described the process of negative reinforcement and how it maintains anxiety, and told him that simply watching the anxiety come and go was all he could really do. I asked him if his anxiety went up when I asked him to pay attention to it, and he replied that it did. I said that this is what it's supposed to do, that this is normal, and that if he continued to watch it directly and not try to escape from it or think of something else, that eventually it will begin to decline again. I asked him to keep watching, keep breathing, keep paying attention and wait for that moment for the anxiety to decline again. After only 3 or 4 minutes, I did notice he had relaxed somewhat, and he confirmed that the anxiety level had slightly decreased. I gave him encouragement and praise for what he had done so far, and asked him to simply continue for a few more minutes. I also asked him to uncross his arms and legs, if he was willing to do so, as this was another form of defensive escape. Again, his anxiety rose briefly, then began to decline until he felt more relaxed and at ease.

At the end of the initial session, when I asked him what his life would be like without anxiety, he replied that he could not even imagine such a thing. He had been anxious so long that it became a part of his identity. However, once he fully grasped the idea that anxiety rises, crests, then falls, he actually got excited about going out and trying new things, better able to simply observe his experiences. After a couple of months, he became a new person.

CASE EXAMPLE: "ANGRY FACE"

Mindfulness brings awareness. I (RWS) once worked with a man at a residential clinic in a hospital who had lived a difficult life. He had been in the military, had been in prison, and had been homeless for several years. In order to survive in the tough environments he lived in, he learned to have an angry expression on his face. This expression basically said, "Don't mess with me." However, this face now prevented him from forming friendships and made it difficult for him to secure employment. I brought this to his attention in a psychotherapy session.

Having seen him for several weeks, I knew we had developed some rapport, and I could be direct with him. "You know, I've seen you interact multiple times with the other residents, and I know you are a kind person, but right in this moment, I feel like you want to kill me. Your face looks very angry." He was quite surprised at this, saying that he did not ever notice that about himself, and he even questioned if it was true. I asked him to be more mindful of the expressions on his face in the coming week, by looking in the mirror, and by being aware of the muscle tone in his face.

At the next session, he smiled at me and said, "Wow, I looked in the mirror, and you were right! I didn't know I looked so angry all the time!" From that point forward, he looked much happier around the unit. He now had conscious choice of when it was necessary to look angry, and when it was necessary to look inviting or happy, which served him well in his next job interview.

CASE EXAMPLE: "RECURRENT CRISES"

Tiffany is a 45-year-old single woman, living on her own in a single-bedroom apartment. She began treatment under the recommendation of her psychiatrist, who had been treating her for some time for feelings of intense anxiety and depression because of chronic pain. Approximately 20 years prior to this course of treatment, Tiffany was an aspiring athlete who had to give up her goals of competing in a professional setting due to an injury. She continues to experience pain, and is extremely cautious in any physical activity to avoid further injury.

Tiffany reports recurrent crises in her life, which produce intense feelings of anxiety. During these times her thoughts race, she becomes short of breath, feels her temperature rise, and feels as though she will become "out of control." She stated during the initial stages of treatment that she felt as though she was cheated out of her life, and that she had no hopes of doing anything that she wanted because of her injury. Tiffany would identify her injury as a reason for any problem in her life. She would back away from any challenge due to her anxiety of failure, or out of fear that she might reinjure herself. She relied on Xanax to calm herself at the slightest indication of anxiety.

Tiffany had been through counseling for many years prior to this course of therapy. She always felt as though her therapist was telling her that her pain was "in her head," and that others judged her for the way her life had been for the past 20 years. She asserted that she had "tried everything before," but she enjoyed having time to talk to someone about her difficulties.

Tiffany was presented with the concepts of mindfulness training as a way for her to learn to reengage her life as an active participant, rather than wasting her time "trying to fix something wrong with her." This began when Tiffany started to become anxious in a session and frantically searched for her missing Xanax. While she was caught in her anxious loop, the therapist asked her to begin describing how her body felt as she was becoming anxious. Through that process, she began to come into her body, her thoughts about the Xanax calmed, and she did not need to take the pill.

Tiffany was presented with mindfulness-based activities within the therapy sessions, including the body scan, awareness of breathing, awareness of thoughts and feelings, gentle mindful movement, and basic Yoga poses. Tiffany was given a CD for home practice, emphasizing that mindfulness teaches a way to accept limitations and to be present with each moment of life as it occurs. Throughout treatment, Tiffany became more aware of how she took herself away from her current experience and placed thoughts of the past or fears about the future in its place.

The body scan proved to be an essential component of working with Tiffany. She lived with a great deal of fear of injuring her body, such that she reacted strongly to any sign of discomfort. During the first body scan, Tiffany reported strong bodily pain in her back and neck, becoming preoccupied with that to a degree that she had a hard time identifying sensations in any other part of her body. However, with time she was able to identify areas that did not experience pain. She engaged in this practice each week, was gradually able to let go of her injury focus, and began, independent of therapy, to engage in activities she had thought impossible. She became active in a dance class, where she was able to interact with others, and applied for part-time employment. She started to live more fully within the bounds of the limitations of her injury, without avoiding activities that were well within her abilities. Tiffany noted near the end of treatment that she spent less time on negative thoughts about being a failure. She noticed a decrease in her reliance on Xanax, and her mood seemed to improve.

Tiffany returned to the office approximately 3 months following the end of scheduled sessions. At that time, she presented in a confident manner, stating that she had continued dancing, maintained employment, and had begun a romantic relationship. She attributed the drastic changes to the mindfulness techniques she had learned.

MINDFULNESS IN CLINICAL SUPERVISION

Just as in individual therapy, mindfulness has been used in clinical supervision. Sessions can begin with a brief mindfulness exercise to clear away the mental distractions and get in touch with present-moment experience. Also, by getting in the habit of defusing from thoughts, trainees can learn to pick up subtle feeling states that they may be experiencing with clients.

In their book on clinical supervision, Safran et al. (2008) describe the usefulness of incorporating mindfulness:

> To begin each session, trainees are given some simple mindfulness exercises, such as carefully attending to the sensory experience of eating a raisin (Kabat-Zinn, 1991), focusing on their bodies for a few moments in an attempt to become aware of any physical sensations that emerge and to note when they find their mind wandering, or attending to the breath (following the inhalations and exhalations with attention). These exercises set the tone for each session by focusing trainees' awareness on the present and helping them adopt a sense of nonjudgmental awareness of their own sensory and emotional states.
>
> Over time, this type of mindfulness work helps trainees increase their awareness of subtle feelings, thoughts, and fantasies that emerge when working with their client, which provide important information about what is occurring in the relationship. One of the most valuable by-products of this kind of mindfulness work is a gradual development of a more tolerant and accepting stance toward a full range of internal experiences. In fact, we conceptualize therapeutic metacommunication as a type of mindfulness in action, insofar as it involves reflecting on experience in a relational context as it emerges in the here and now, in an attentive, nonjudgmental fashion (Safran, 2002; Safran & Muran, 2000). (p. 145)

FOR MORE INFORMATION

Eating Mindfully

Albers, S. (2003). *Eating Mindfully: How to End Mindless Eating and Enjoy a Balanced Relationship With Food.* Oakland, CA: New Harbinger Publications. A full-length book written for the lay reader, filled with principles and exercises to bring mindfulness to the process of eating.

Open Mind Training

Alexander, R. (2008). *Wise Mind, Open Mind: Finding Purpose and Meaning in Times of Crisis, Loss, & Change.* Oakland, CA: New Harbinger Publications. A very readable book that outlines the three-step process of opening up to creativity using mindfulness.

Mindful Recovery

Bien, T., & Bien, B. (2002). *Mindful Recovery: A Spiritual Path to Healing From Addiction.* New York: John Wiley & Sons. An inspiring book written for the lay reader who is struggling with addiction.

Chapter 9

Future Directions

The explosion of popularity with mindfulness-based interventions is exciting. Because of the solid initial research, mindfulness-based interventions have been growing in acceptance in the professional community and the public.

However, there are times when the zeal of practitioners gets ahead of the empirical research. Many clinicians use the word "mindfulness" loosely, and presenters sometimes tack the word onto their seminar titles without thorough integration. Though the foundations and mechanisms of mindfulness are grounded in solid psychological principles, much more research is needed before we can confidently apply these techniques to broader populations and presenting problems.

Of course, there is always a dilemma in this endeavor. Good research requires structured protocols and a homogenous group with a single presenting issue. However, in actual clinical practice, there is a need for flexibility with individual clients with a complicated mix of issues. A good scientist-practitioner balances knowledge of effective principles with the art of doing good therapy in the moment.

In this chapter, we will put forth suggestions for future applications and research. We will investigate two themes: refinement of research and exploration of other forms of meditation that show promise as clinical interventions.

NEED FOR FURTHER RESEARCH

Recent meta-analyses (Burke, 2010; Hofmann et al., 2010) have demonstrated that mindfulness is an effective intervention for depression and anxiety. However, more detailed analyses are needed to determine the specific factors and conditions that are helpful, and to find out what other applications and settings may also benefit from a mindfulness-based intervention. More research on diversity variables and social justice issues is also needed.

REFINEMENT OF FORMAT

Although research to date on established mindfulness protocols has shown good or promising results, future research will need to focus on refinement of the therapeutic factors. For example, is there a dose-response relationship? Most mindfulness groups are held for eight sessions – would 12 sessions be more effective? Would four sessions be enough? Are 2- or 3-hour sessions necessary, or would 1-hour or 5-hour groups be better?

Some ACT therapists talk about mindfulness without meditation (e.g., Harris, 2009). While admitting that formal practice can be very helpful, they recognize that many clients will not practice formally, and yet still teach mindfulness skills with good results. Further research needs to be done to determine the optimal amount of homework practice, or the most effective way to teach incorporation of mindfulness skills into daily life without formal practice.

Perhaps most importantly, are there other factors that account for the phenomenon we are calling mindfulness? The ACT model (see Chapter 6) considers mindfulness to be the combination of defusion, acceptance, contact with the present moment, and self as context (Harris, 2009). Van Dam et al. (2011) found that self-compassion appears to be an important component of MBIs. Future research is necessary to determine if it is useful to keep mindfulness as a meta-construct.

EXPANSION OF POPULATIONS AND SETTINGS

Mindfulness-based interventions are increasingly being developed for different populations and for a wider variety of presenting issues. Below are a few interventions that are in the more exploratory stages.

Organizational Settings

Mental health professionals are uniquely qualified to contribute to the health of organizations (Sears, Rudisill, & Mason-Sears, 2006). By influencing organizations, therapists can expand their influence beyond what they can do in individual and group formats.

Though one does not have to earn an MBA to do good work in organizational settings, it is nonetheless important to learn the vocabulary of the business world. For instance, most executives are more comfortable talking about their "reactions" than about their "feelings."

Peter Senge teaches a method to organizations and executives called "presence" (Senge et al., 2004). The principles are very similar to those found in mindfulness-based interventions. Senge teaches individuals to develop three openings: opening of the mind, opening of the heart, and opening of the will. He refers to the state in which thoughts are cleared out as "suspension." This open state is a source of creativity.

Daniel Goleman and Jon Kabat-Zinn (2007) discuss the use of mindfulness in organizational settings in a conversation available on CD called "Mindfulness @ Work." Kabat-Zinn relates a story of a talk he was giving to a group of executives. He began by saying "let's just sit for a few minutes with no agenda." To his surprise, several of them began weeping. When he asked them about it later, they explained that they always had an agenda. Executives often get stuck in the "doing" mode. However, without taking daily time out for themselves, what Stephen Covey (2004) calls "sharpening the saw," they are at risk for burnout.

Business executives, especially middle management, often suffer from stress and burnout (Sears et al., 2006). According to an article from the *Journal of Management* (Danna & Griffin, 1999), "U.S. industry loses approximately 550 million working days annually to absenteeism, with an estimated 54 percent of these absences being stress-related. Estimates place the annual cost at more than $43 billion" (p. 377). MBSR appears well suited to use in organizational settings, though adaptations appear to be helpful (K. Williams, 2006). One of the authors (RWS) is currently working to adapt MBSR and MBCT into a format that is more readily useful in organizational settings, in a program called M-BOLD (mindfulness-based organizational and leadership development).

Acceptance and commitment therapy has also been applied in organizational settings (e.g., Bond & Flaxman, 2006; Bond, S. C. Hayes, & Barnes-Homes, 2006; Haas & S. C. Hayes, 2006; S. C. Hayes, Bunting, et al., 2006; O'Hora & Maglieri, 2006; Stewart et al., 2006).

Flaxman and Bond (2006) describe the goals of a three-session program of stress management training based on the ACT model:

Session One (3 hours long):
1. To undermine the effectiveness of experiential avoidance strategies.
2. To show that in the realm of thoughts and emotions, control is the problem, not the solution.
3. To introduce psychological acceptance, or mindfulness, as the alternative to experiential avoidance.

Session Two (1 week later, 3 hours long)
1. For participants to clarify their values as chosen life directions and to distinguish values from goals and actions.
2. To help participants contact the "observing self," as distinct from their psychological content (self as context).
3. To introduce additional defusion and mindfulness exercises.
4. To clarify the link between mindfulness and behavioral movement in valued directions.

Session Three (3 months later, 3 hours long)
1. To provide a booster session for mindfulness skills.
2. To discuss any barriers to valued action.
3. To further highlight the link between mindfulness and valued action. (pp. 384, 388, 392)*

Mindful Leadership

Business leaders today are facing tremendous pressures to perform in a very competitive business environment. It can be very challenging to balance the needs of diverse stakeholders, including the environment of the Earth itself. The Center for Mindfulness in Medicine, Health Care, and Society at the University of Massachusetts Medical Center offers Mindful Leadership programs (Center for Mindfulness, n.d.). The courses utilize mindfulness to enhance the skills and attitudes that are important for leaders to embody. Participants are taught to become aware of automatic reactions, increase awareness of self and others, enhance empathic communication, create space to develop creativity, and develop emotional resilience.

---

* From "Acceptance and Commitment Therapy in the Workplace" by P. E. Flaxman and F. W. Bond, 2006, in R. Baer (Ed.), *Mindfulness-Based Treatment Approaches: Clinician's Guide to Evidence Base and Applications*, pp. 377-402. Copyright © 2006 by Elsevier. Reprinted with permission.

Executive Coaching

Executive and life coaching is popular among business executives and other individuals who are looking to improve themselves and their performance in life and on the job (Fitzgerald & Berger, 2002; Flaherty, 1999; Hargrove, 1995; Hargrove & Kaestner, 1998; Kilburg, 2000; J. Miller & Brown, 1993; Sears et al., 2006). Properly trained mental health professionals are especially well suited for coaching because of our training in interpersonal skills. We are also skilled at assessing an individual's performance within the context of a larger system, and at giving constructive and sometimes delicate feedback (Sears et al., 2006).

"Coaching is a one-on-one relationship, taking place as an ongoing process (involving multiple sessions), which focuses on improving an individual's insight into his or her own functioning and on improving his or her effectiveness in an organization (Kraiger, 2002; Peterson, 2002)" (Sears et al., 2006, p. 155). In contrast to therapy, the focus is future and goal oriented, removing obstacles to accomplishment, and does not focus on psychopathology.

Mindfulness techniques are likely to be useful in executive and life coaching. Coaches can begin sessions with a 3-minute breathing space to set the tone of the session, just as a mindfulness group facilitator does. A coach can also ask the client to take a few breaths anytime the client becomes anxious.

One of the authors (RWS) is currently developing a mindfulness program for individual development known as M-POWER (mindfulness-based personal optimization with emotional resilience).

Although mindfulness in organizational settings is based upon techniques that have empirical support, much more research is needed to clarify the benefits and to establish the best methods of instruction.

DIVERSITY ISSUES

In the early days of psychology and psychiatry, the major influencers were white males. As Robert Guthrie (2003) so poignantly stated in the title of his book on the history of psychology, *Even the Rat was White.*

Although there are some significant exceptions (e.g., S. C. Hayes, 2007; Ting-Toomey, 2009; Vacarr, 2001), in general, there is a dearth of research investigating diversity variables in mindfulness-based interventions. Diversity is recognized as an important competency in the mental health fields, and state boards can sanction a clinician who operates outside of his or her competencies.

In addition to further research on diversity variables in mindfulness research, clinicians can bring mindful awareness to bear on their own sensitivity to matters of diversity. For instance, all of us can at times engage in unconscious acts of discrimination or can commit microaggressions (Sue et al., 2007):

> Racial microaggressions are brief and commonplace daily verbal, behavioral, and environmental indignities, whether intentional or unintentional, that communicate hostile, derogatory, or negative racial slights and insults to the target person or group. They are not limited to human encounters alone but may also be environmental in nature, as when a person of color is exposed to an office setting that unintentionally assails his or her racial identity (Gordon & Johnson, 2003; D. W. Sue, 2003). . . . Three forms of microaggressions can be identified: microassault, microinsult, and microinvalidation.
>
> A microassault is an explicit racial derogation characterized primarily by a verbal or nonverbal attack meant to hurt the intended victim through name-calling, avoidant behavior, or purposeful discriminatory actions.
>
> A microinsult is characterized by communications that convey rudeness and insensitivity and demean a person's racial heritage or identity. Microinsults represent subtle snubs, frequently unknown to the perpetrator, but clearly convey a hidden insulting message to the recipient of color.
>
> Microinvalidations are characterized by communications that exclude, negate, or nullify the psychological thoughts, feelings, or experiential reality of a person of color. When Asian Americans (born and raised in the United States) are complimented for speaking good English or are repeatedly asked where they were born, the effect is to negate their U.S. American heritage and to convey that they are perpetual foreigners. When Blacks are told that "I don't see color" or "We are all human beings," the effect is to negate their experiences as racial/cultural beings (Helms, 1992). (pp. 273-274)

It can be very difficult at times to openly discuss matters of diversity, because we open ourselves up to potential conflict and to the possibility that we still hold on to our own subtle biases. Mindfulness can be an anchor to help us speak up when necessary to call out discriminatory words and behaviors for what they are and to be open and accepting of our own issues.

SOCIAL JUSTICE ISSUES

Moving beyond an understanding of individual and cultural differences, social justice involves the responsibility of using our power and influence as change makers to make the world a more fair and tolerant place. Fouad, Gerstein, and Toporek (2006) describe social justice as follows:

> Related to the legal notion of equity for all within the law, social justice also connotes that the distribution of advantages be fair and equitable to all individuals, regardless of race, gender, ability status, sexual orientation, physical makeup, or religious creed. (p. 1)

Mental health professionals are uniquely qualified to have an impact on organizations and communities through consultation and advocacy efforts (Sears et al., 2006). Not speaking up when we witness discrimination is a subtle form of condoning it.

Mindfulness appears to be an ideal tool for creating change in the world. By embodying mindfulness and acceptance in ourselves, we serve as models to inspire others. Mindfulness provides a clarity that is necessary to understand how things are, which is necessary before we take action to facilitate change. Imagine a society transformed by mindful awareness, wherein we promote better relationships with ourselves, our communities, and our environment.

MOVING BEYOND MINDFULNESS: EXPLORATION OF OTHER FORMS OF MEDITATION

Meditation has been practiced throughout the world by nearly every culture, for thousands of years. The collective wisdom of millions of human beings exploring the human mind is likely to contain great treasures. However, sometimes things are passed along that contain purely cultural influences, or the methods are effective for reasons other than those traditionally taught. Although we must be careful not to dismiss methods that sometimes require a lifetime of training to fully understand, we can also apply the lens of science to develop expedient means for helping to reduce suffering in the modern world. In this section, we will explore a few types of meditation that appear to hold promise as clinical interventions.

THE FOURTH FOUNDATION OF MINDFULNESS

As mentioned in Chapter 1, there are traditionally four foundations of mindfulness. Although the first three foundations (mindfulness of form, feelings, and thoughts) are so far being used effectively in clinical practice, we believe that the fourth area holds great potential for moving beyond mindfulness to therapeutic exercises for letting go of our self-inflicted suffering and finding deeper happiness in our lives.

The fourth foundation is mindfulness of external things, or of the nature of reality. According to this tradition, reality is marked by the qualities of impermanence, interdependence, and lack of any solid, unchanging self. For example, this involves remembering not to confuse names and words with reality – we say "car," like it's a thing, but there is no essence of car. A car is composed of parts that are themselves composed of smaller, replaceable components.

Below, we discuss methods and topics for this fourth foundation of mindfulness, as well as several other meditative methods.

STOPPING AND SEEING

Chih-I (b. 538 CE) was a great synthesizer of ancient meditation traditions. He propagated a meditation method known in Chinese as Chih-Kuan (Japanese Shi-Kan), which means "stopping and seeing" (Cleary, 1997). "Stopping" is similar to the Transcendental Meditation method whereby one clears one's mind. "Seeing" is similar to the method of mindfulness, or insight meditation, whereby one discerns the nature of reality. Chih-I taught that these two methods should be

止	觀
Chih	Kuan
Shi	Kan
Dhyana	Prajna
Samatha	Vipassana
Stopping	Seeing
Clear	Insight

used together. If one has difficulty clearing one's mind, one can analyze the contents of one's thoughts. If one's mind wanders when looking at the nature of things, one can go back to clearing the mind of thoughts.

Listed on page 150 are the different terminologies used for Stopping (left column) and Seeing (right column).

Shi-kan meditation is an excellent foundation from which to contemplate the nature of reality. Below are some suggested exercises for developing this skill.

Exercise

This meditation is to develop the *shi*, or "stopping" meditation, in which you allow the proliferation of random thoughts to stop. Light a candle and place it at least an arm's length away from you. Assume whatever posture you find comfortable. For a 10- to 20-minute period, look directly at the flame. Put your entire attention on the flame. If anything enters your mind that is not the flame, let it go and return to your concentration. Allow yourself a feeling of ease and gentleness.

Exercise

This meditation is to develop the *kan*, or "seeing" meditation, also known as insight or analytical meditation, in which you sharpen your mind to look at the true nature of something. Light a candle and place it at least an arm's length away from you. Assume whatever posture you find comfortable. For a 10- to 20-minute period, look directly at the flame. Analyze exactly what a flame is, where it comes from, what causes and conditions bring it into existence, and so on. Don't settle for surface level answers. Go beneath the mind's tendency to classify and move on. Allow yourself creativity, but keep the flame as the topic of your thoughts. If you wish, you can philosophically apply your insights to yourself and the world around you at another time.

Exercise

This meditation is to allow *shi* and *kan* to work together. Light a candle and place it at least an arm's length away from you. Assume whatever posture you find comfortable. For a 10- to 20-minute period, look directly at the flame. Begin by practicing *shi*. When the mind is calm and concentrated, practice *kan*. If your mind wanders, or your analytical thinking feels as though it has reached a dead end, return to practicing *shi*. Alternate your use of *shi* and *kan* as appropriate.

Exercise

In many mindfulness courses, one practices *shi* on the breath to develop concentration. In this meditation, you will use *kan* on the breath. Assume whatever posture you find comfortable. For a silent 10- to 20-minute period, you will analyze the process of breathing. Use all of your senses. Note the feeling of your muscles and ribs, the air as it moves through your nose and lungs, and so on. Also think about where the air comes from, how so many other beings share the same air, how it becomes a part of you through the medium of your blood, and so forth.

Exercise

In this meditation, you will practice both *shi* and *kan* on the breath. Assume whatever posture you find comfortable. For a 10- to 20-minute period, concern yourself only with your breath. Begin by using *shi* on the breath to calm and concentrate the mind, either by counting the breaths or simply by focusing on the breath with a clear mind. When you feel ready, use *kan* to develop insight into the process of breathing. When the mind strays from the subject, bring it back by using *shi* to concentrate on the breath.

Exercise

In this meditation, you can apply *kan* to any topic you wish. It can be spiritual, such as analyzing where the feeling of being an isolated self comes from, or it can be mundane, such as how to efficiently fix something that was broken. Or it can be both, such as analyzing where your own insecurities are when you get angry at something or someone else. Whenever your mind gets too far off the subject, return to *shi* by meditating on the breath, or simply keep your mind in a clear state empty of verbal thoughts. When the mind is clear, return to your subject with *kan*.

MEDITATION ON IMPERMANENCE, INTERDEPENDENCE, AND EMPTINESS

We all long to hold on to happy times, loved ones, and treasured possessions, but the truth is, nothing lasts forever. In fact, we *cannot* hold on to anything, even if we try. The world is continuously changing. Our attempt to grasp onto things is what causes our frustration and suffering. Once this insight is internalized, not just intellectually, but as a *feeling*, we can begin to let go of our struggles with life, and enjoy each moment as the gift that it is.

McDonald and Courtin (2005) give a description of a meditation on impermanence that begins with contemplation of one's internal environment. The meditator is asked to contemplate the ever-changing nature of the physiology and cells of the body, as well as the ephemeral nature of thoughts and the mind. Next, they invite the meditator to contemplate the impermanence of the external world, starting with the nearby environment, eventually including all living and nonliving things in the world. The meditator is encouraged to hold on to the sense that all things are constantly changing, even if only at a subtle, molecular level. One is encouraged to recognize the futility of grasping at what is by nature impermanent.

At a deeper level, one realizes that things are impermanent because they are ever-changing. They are ever-changing because they are interdependent, meaning each person or "thing" depends on countless other conditions to exist. The tree outside my window depends on sunlight, moisture, air, and the earth. Sunlight depends on all of the astronomical processes it took to produce the sun. Moisture depends on the water cycle, which depends on evaporation of the oceans, movements of the air, and so on. Recognizing this interdependence leads to the realization that all things are "empty" of inherent self-existence. Life becomes a fluid dance instead of a struggle of Newtonian billiard balls.

To put it less poetically, such contemplations can lead to increased psychological flexibility and lead to behavioral activation toward valued goals.

MEDITATION ON DEATH

Death is rarely studied systematically in clinical training, but often comes up in therapy. Being able to address death directly with clients is important for therapists and can lead to a greater appreciation of life.

Death (or more symbolically, "change") is an important factor in the existential psychotherapeutic tradition (Yalom, 1980). Physical death is guaranteed to occur to every human being without exception and, hence, can create a great deal of anxiety (Florian & Mikulincer, 2004). However, modern society in general rarely speaks about death.

Clients often come to psychotherapy after the loss of a loved one because friends and relatives are uncomfortable with how to relate to death, often telling the grieving person to "get over it" or "get on with their lives."

With certain notable exceptions (e.g., Becker, 1998; Freud, 1963; Kubler-Ross, 1997; Yalom, 1980), modern society has historically not prepared people very well for the inevitability of death, and most individuals try to avoid talking or thinking about it. Hence, when death does come, people are unprepared to process it. Although being educated about death does not remove the pain of separation from a loved one, a little preparation does go a long way in helping one through the grieving process. Certain circumstances, such as diagnosis of a family member with a terminal illness, involve a significant strain on emotional and financial resources, and Sogyal Rinpoche (2002) recommends not contemplating death when one is under emotional strain. However, preparation can help one to grieve fully (whatever that means to the individual or culture) without adding additional anxiety or worries about the grieving itself.

In the Eastern wisdom traditions, death is highlighted prominently (Kapleau, 1989; McDonald & Courtin, 2005; Rinpoche, 2002). In the Buddhist tradition, for instance, there are a set of contemplation exercises designed to help one prepare for death and thereby, to more fully appreciate life. For modern societies, this may seem somewhat morbid, and may remind clinicians of the obsessive thoughts about death seen in those who are severely depressed. But in the East, this is a liberating type of experience. By facing this inevitability head on, in a type of exposure therapy, it loses its artificially inflated ability to provoke anxiety.

Importantly, in the Eastern traditions, one is told not to do the meditations on death if one is feeling depressed (Rinpoche, 2002). One needs to be in a stable affective state in order to get the most benefit from these meditations. Just as one becomes a safer driver after having an automobile accident and recognizing that the dangers of driving are not merely abstract concepts, an individual may live life a little bit differently knowing how fragile it is.

In the East, death is meditated upon systematically. There are several components to this contemplation process. One is the idea of the universality of death (McDonald & Courtin, 2005; Rinpoche, 2002). One considers that all living creatures, without exception (including oneself), will one day die. This includes all loved ones, all pets, everyone who has ever lived or will ever live.

Another component of the contemplation practice is to consider the inevitability of death (McDonald & Courtin, 2005; Rinpoche, 2002). In this phase, one considers that there is no escape from death. This is important, as many individuals feel that certain people will always be in their lives. Even those who are fabulously wealthy can still get sick or die of cancer; even the most brilliant person can die in a car accident. There is no one in the world who has ever permanently cheated death, no one whom death has simply forgotten about.

Another consideration is that one does not know when death will occur (McDonald & Courtin, 2005; Rinpoche, 2002). Sometimes children die before parents do. Sometimes babies die in their cribs. Not knowing when death will occur keeps one more appreciative of this moment, for the time that one does have to live.

A further consideration is that one does not know the manner of one's death (McDonald & Courtin, 2005; Rinpoche, 2002). A person could die peacefully while sleeping, or die slowly and painfully of cancer.

In Western Existential psychotherapy, death is one of the "four givens" of human existence (Schneider, 2003; Yalom, 1980). By facing these existential truths directly, one becomes inoculated to the anxiety that grows from avoidance of these issues. One is then freed to appreciate each moment of life as it unfolds and to create a meaningful existence.

Death is rarely talked about in our school systems, but age-appropriate education about death (e.g., Coder, 2004) may also be helpful to begin to make the topic more acceptable and less uncomfortable.

By becoming more aware of and comfortable with death and change, clinicians may be able to be more fully present with clients as they face this inevitable given of life. However, controlled studies are needed to verify the usefulness of systematically contemplating death.

LOVING-KINDNESS
AND COMPASSION

The same Eastern traditions that developed mindfulness meditation also developed loving-kindness and compassion meditations. These exercises can be used to counter the feeling of isolation, competition, cynicism, and lack of connection so prevalent in modern society.

Tulku Thondup (2008) describes the 12 stages of a traditional practice designed to foster loving-kindness:

1. Develop the right attitude.
2. Bring the mind back to the body.
3. Visualize an image that represents the embodiment of loving-kindness.
4. Connect to the image with sound (e.g., om mani padme hung).
5. Visualize receiving light and loving-kindness.
6. Visualize, imagine, and feel your body transforming into light.
7. Allow the light-energy to move in waves through your body.
8. Amplify the waves with sound (e.g., "Ahhhh").
9. Offer loving-kindness to a loved one.
10. Offer loving-kindness to others and to all.
11. Rest in the awareness of loving-kindness.
12. Dedicate your practice to others and aspire to continue the practice. (Adapted from Thondup, 2008, pp. 109-111)

Though Thondup writes about the traditional Tibetan Buddhist practice, we believe there may be potential in adapting it for a wider audience.

Salzberg (1995) describes the traditional phrases used in a meditation to develop loving-kindness toward oneself:

"May I be free from danger."
"May I have mental happiness."
"May I have physical happiness."
"May I have ease of well-being." (p. 30)

In the formal practice, one begins with feeling loving-kindness and compassion toward oneself, then toward loved ones, then toward strangers, then toward so-called enemies, until one can feel the entire world enveloped in loving-kindness.

Subjectively, this results in a dropping of anger, defenses, and negativity, leading to more compassionate activity in the world. From the ACT point of view, this appears to lead to increased psychological flexibility. Although initial research on compassion and self-compassion appears promising (e.g., Gilbert, 2009; Gilbert & Procter, 2006; Kelly et al., 2010; Tirch, 2010; Van Dam et al., 2011), more research is needed to evaluate the effectiveness of this formal practice.

A meditation on loving-kindness is provided on track 5 of the CD included with this volume.

TAKING ON NEGATIVITY

In the Tibetan tradition, a practice was developed - known as tonglen - which literally means "giving and receiving" (Rinpoche, 2002, p. 197). It is a method used to loosen constricted ideas of the self and promote compassion. It is often used as a way of giving meaning to those who are sick; that is, it helps one to move away from a self-centered perspective. For instance, I (RWS) used this exercise for a cancer support group, and the participants reported finding it helpful.

This practice can be done while visualizing a sick person, or by visualizing all of the ills of the world. Breathing in, you imagine yourself inhaling black smoke, which represents all the sickness and negativity in the world (or in the person you are imagining). This smoke is transformed inside your body, and you exhale bright, white, sparkling light back out into the world (or to the individual you are imagining).

Tonglen may seem counterintuitive – when you are sick, to imagine taking on more. However, as with mindfulness, there is likely a component of exposure therapy. It may also serve to increase psychological flexibility, by having the mind exercise a different way of relating to a problem. Further research is needed on the effectiveness of this approach, especially with clinical populations.

ZEN

Many have written about Zen and therapy (e.g., Austin, 1998; Bein, 2008; Birx, 2002; Brazier, 1995; Fromm, Suzuki, & DeMartino, 1960; Martin, 1999; Pawle, 2008; Rosenbaum, 1999; Watts, 1961). Although we don't feel it is likely (or necessary) to fully develop a systematic, self-contained "Zen Therapy," we feel that there are many concepts and techniques employed by Zen that may be useful in a psychotherapeutic context.

Zen is the Japanese way of pronouncing the Chinese word Ch'an, which is a transliteration of the Sanskrit word Dhyana, which literally translated refers to "meditation" (Watts, 1957). There is a classic four-line description of Zen, attributed to Bodhidharma:

教 外 別 伝
不 立 文 字
直 指 人 心
見 性 成 仏

Outside teachings, a special transmission.
Not dependent on words.
Direct pointing to the human mind.
Self-awareness, becoming awakened.

Zen grew out of the Buddhist tradition, and it emphasizes direct experience over philosophical speculation. The late Zen master Seung Sahn emphasized the importance of a "don't know mind," a state which is open to direct experience. He talks about reality being "like this," meaning that we don't need to add intellectual interpretation. Likewise, Shunryu Suzuki (2006) writes about the concept of "beginner's mind," which is open to all possibilities. Similar to ACT, Zen teaches not to confuse thoughts with reality.

A Zen master might warn of a danger in mindfulness, asking "Who is being mindful?" If you separate yourself from what you are being mindful of, you will get in your own way, much like performers often mess themselves up when their conscious thinking gets in the way. I (RWS) remember riding my bicycle, knowing someone was holding on to me, then looking back, noticing that my older sister had indeed let go, and immediately falling. I also remember playing guitar for an audience, feeling that the music was playing by itself, then getting in my own way by trying to think about it and messing up. Zen training helps to let go of this excessive self-consciousness, to see and act more directly.

Zen often teaches through direct exchanges with a teacher. Lynch (2006) gives some examples of the kinds of exchanges students can have with Zen teachers:

When the student enters the interview room; the teacher places a cup and a pen on the floor and asks if the cup and the pen are the same or different. The four kinds of "like this" answers could be:

- Without like this: maintain complete silence, a don't know mind.
- Become one like this: hit the floor or shout KATZ!
- Only like this: saying "cup is cup, pen is pen."
- Just like this: drink from the cup, write with the pen. (p. 21)

Some Zen systems use a systematic training tool known as the "koan" or "kong-an," which translates as "public case," as they often involve stories about Zen teachers and their students. The koans are designed to hook the student with a problem that only exists in the student's mind, not in reality. Hence, the problem seems unsolvable until the student lets go of his or her conditioned way of looking at things.

Reggie Pawle (2008) uses a method he calls "koan therapy," which involves finding and clearly defining the seemingly unsolvable problems in clients' lives and having them sit with the problems until they can be related to in a new way.

Tomio Hirai (1989), a Japanese psychiatrist, has studied and written about the therapeutic effects of Zen meditation. Hirai has done extensive studies of Zen priests performing shikantaza formless meditation, and has found distinct electroencephalogram (EEG) signatures characterized by alpha and theta waves. Hirai posits that Zen meditation has therapeutic value for those who practice it, especially for those suffering from anxiety.

Hirai (1989) tells the story of a famous television reporter visiting a Zen priest in Japan. Both the priest and the reporter were connected to EEG and other physiological recording devices. After 10 minutes of meditation, a lovely, young, bikini-clad woman came into the room and sat down across from them. The reporter showed quite a bit of physiological reaction, but the priest showed almost none.

Next, the crew dropped a realistic-looking rubber snake from the ceiling. Even though he was in on the joke, the reporter showed EEG disturbances that lasted for a while. The priest showed a momentary reaction, but quickly returned to equilibrium.

Hirai quotes the priest as saying, ". . . this is the meaning of not being obsessed. Although I am a trained Zen priest, the appearance of a beautiful young girl in a bathing suit and the sudden dropping down of a snake are stimuli to which I react. This is proof of the awareness during the Zazen state. But I was able to return to a normal state of tranquility quickly" (Hirai, 1989, p. 153).

This is one of the goals of Zen training: to react appropriately in the moment, but not to linger too long over things in a constructed mental world. This is why Hirai (1989) believes that Zen training can be useful for anxiety, which is maintained through ruminations and worries.

It is important to keep in mind that Zen and psychotherapy have different purposes and goals. However, psychotherapy may gain important insights from this ancient tradition. Of course, more systematic research is necessary to demonstrate clinical benefits.

THE PATH OF THE DIAMOND THUNDERBOLT

As mentioned in Chapter 1, the Japanese and Tibetan traditions have a method known as the *vajrayana*, which is the culmination of all the Buddhist teachings. This method is considered the short path to enlightenment, as it works to transform all of our experiences into tools for awakening. This path has, until recently, been kept hidden or secret, as the techniques are considered dangerous if misused (S. K. Hayes, 1993, 2000).

This approach involves the alignment of thoughts, words, and actions. To become a compassionate person, one must think, speak, and act compassionately. To aid in the development of these three areas, one engages in symbolic actions. One visualizes images that evoke compassion, or imagines oneself as the ideal embodiment of compassion. One speaks words that reflect a deep feeling of compassion. One also engages in bodily gestures that convey compassion. By programming our body, speech, and mind in this way, we can more effectively embody these qualities in the world. This is similar to the Adlerian idea of "as if," or the colloquial saying, "Fake it till you make it."

Many clients come to therapy feeling empty, or embody a negative sense of self. These exercises can be used to practice being more resolute, more compassionate, more loving, and so on. From an ACT point of view, trying on new personas can increase psychological flexibility and empowers a person to move in valued directions. From a dialectical point of view, clients realize that they are not stuck in one identity – they have within them the potential to embody a myriad of qualities, which can all be effectively integrated. Ultimately, the restricted sense of self is let go, leading to what ACT calls "self as context," instead of confusing who we are with the content of our thoughts.

Reinventing one's self is also akin to what is done in Narrative Therapy. I (RWS) once had a client at a university counseling center who was very depressed. He was in danger of failing his courses if he did not attend his upcoming exams, but he felt averse to going. His mother finally talked him into coming to see me. The client told me that all he wanted to do was sit in his dorm room and watch fantasy movies, where he felt the world made more sense. He knew he needed to go to class, but felt he couldn't overcome his fears. Drawing on my own love of the *Lord of the Rings* trilogy (Tolkien, 1994), which the client immediately identified with, I related his predicament to the hobbit Frodo in need of destroying the evil ring. The ring could not be ignored, and could not be hidden, as the forces of evil would come and find it. It could only be destroyed in the fires of Mt. Doom, where it was made. Likewise, he could not ignore his classes and grades, or he would be kicked out of school. I asked him to imagine the grounds of the campus as the hellish land of Mordor, across which he had to venture to get to Mt. Doom (the classroom). The client seemed very inspired by this image, and later reported that he had brought all of his grades up and was doing well. The image of being a more powerful, determined person gave him the motivation to shift out of the downward spiral in which he had been stuck.

Of course, controlled research is necessary to determine the most effective way of using these methods therapeutically. Interestingly, even traditional practitioners recognize that all of the methods of the *vajrayana* are expedient means. Consider the following, excerpted from a private commentary on the *Rishu-kyo*, the "Wisdom Truth Teachings":

> Although these categories are created to explain things, ultimately, all individual categories are false. The six great elements, the four mandalas, the three secrets, and so forth, do not really exist. Those categories are aids. They are devices used for the sake of practice. In the vajrayana, the practice itself is the end. This is the same idea as in

Zen practice. Therefore, the accomplished practitioner is able to discard these categories and the devices they contain, and simply be awake.

Likewise, modern clinical practitioners are advised to be careful not to make mindfulness itself an end goal, or to make it some kind of sacred thing, or to become a "militant for mindfulness." The history of psychology is already too full of competing cult-like schools of thought. After we cross a river using a raft, we don't need to carry the raft around on our backs all the time, and we don't need to preach to others why they too should all carry rafts on their backs. There is no need to become attached to the concept of mindfulness – it is simply a concept that describes a natural human process.

Mindfulness is a tool we can use for ourselves and for our clients to wake up to the present moment. When you put this book down, ask yourself, "What am I experiencing right now?" When you meet with a client, ask, "How may I help you?"

FOR MORE INFORMATION

Buddhist Meditation Practices

McDonald, K., & Courtin, R. (2005). *How to Meditate: A Practical Guide* (2nd ed). Boston: Wisdom Publications. This book covers a wide variety of meditative techniques, with practical instructions for doing each of them. Though written from a Buddhist perspective, we see a number of potential clinical applications.

Zen Meditation

Suzuki, S. (2006). *Zen Mind, Beginner's Mind.* Boston: Shambhala Publications. This book contains delightful, short chapters, which are the collected talks of Zen master Shunryu Suzuki on Zen meditation.

Vajrayana

Blue Lotus Assembly (http://www.bluelotusassembly.org/). This organization, headed by Stephen K. Hayes, translates the teachings of the Vajrayana tradition into practical, modern methods for daily living. Also see the website of Stephen K. Hayes (http://www.stephenkhayes.com/).

References

Albers, S. (2003). *Eating Mindfully: How to End Mindless Eating and Enjoy a Balanced Relationship With Food*. Oakland, CA: New Harbinger Publications.

Albers, S. (2006). *Mindful Eating 101: A Guide to Healthy Eating in College and Beyond*. New York: Routledge.

Albers, S. (2008). *Eat, Drink, and Be Mindful*. Oakland, CA: New Harbinger Publications.

Albers, S. (2009). *50 Ways to Soothe Yourself Without Food*. Oakland, CA: New Harbinger Publications.

Alexander, R. (2008). *Wise Mind, Open Mind: Finding Purpose and Meaning in Times of Crisis, Loss, & Change*. Oakland, CA: New Harbinger Publications.

American Psychiatric Association. (2000). *Diagnostic and Statistical Manual of Mental Disorders* (4th ed. text rev.). Washington, DC: Author.

Astin, J. A. (1997). Stress reduction through mindfulness meditation: Effects on psychological symptomatology, sense of control, and spiritual experiences. *Psychotherapy and Psychosomatics, 66*, 97-106.

Atwood, J. D., & Maltin, L. (1994). Putting eastern philosophies into western psychotherapies. *American Journal of Psychotherapy, XLV* (3).

Austin, J. H. (1998). *Zen and the Brain: Toward an Understanding of Meditation and Consciousness*. Cambridge, MA: MIT Press.

Bach, P., & Hayes, S. C. (2002). The use of Acceptance and Commitment Therapy to prevent the rehospitalization of psychotic patients: A randomized controlled trial. *Journal of Consulting and Clinical Psychology, 70*, 1129-1139.

Baer, R. (2003). Mindfulness training as a clinical intervention: A conceptual and empirical review. *Clinical Psychology: Science and Practice, 10*(2), 125-143. doi:10.1093/clipsy/bpg015.

Baer, R. (Ed.). (2006). *Mindfulness-Based Treatment Approaches: Clinician's Guide to Evidence Base and Applications*. Burlington, MA: Academic Press.

Barnard, P. J., & Teasdale, J. D. (1991). Interacting cognitive subsystems: A systemic approach to cognitive-affective interaction and change. *Cognition and Emotion, 5*, 1-39.

Barnes, S., Brown, K., Krusemark, E., Campbell, W. K., & Rogge, R. D. (2007). The role of mindfulness in romantic relationship satisfaction and responses to relationship stress. *Journal of Marital and Family Therapy, 33*(4), 482-500.

Beck, A. T., Rush, A. J., Shaw, B. F., & Emery, G. (1979). *Cognitive Therapy of Depression.* New York: Guilford Press.

Becker, E. (1998). *The Denial of Death.* New York: Free Press Paperbacks.

Behavioral Tech. (2010). *DBT Resources: What is DBT?* Retrieved from http://www.behavioraltech.com/resources/whatisdbt.cfm

Bein, A. (2008). *The Zen of Helping: Spiritual Principles for Mindful and Open-Hearted Practice.* New York: John Wiley & Sons.

Benson, H., & Klipper, M. (1975). *The Relaxation Response.* New York: Avon Books.

Biegel, G., Brown, K., Shapiro, S., & Schubert, C. (2009). Mindfulness-based stress reduction for treatment of adolescent psychiatric outpatients: A randomized clinical trial. *Journal of Counseling and Clinical Psychology, 77*(5), 855-866.

Bien, T. (2006). *Mindful Therapy: A Guide for Therapists and Helping Professionals.* Boston: Wisdom Publications.

Bien, T., & Bien, B. (2002). *Mindful Recovery: A Spiritual Path to Healing From Addiction.* New York: John Wiley & Sons.

Biglan, A., & Hayes, S. C. (1996). Should the behavioral sciences become more pragmatic? The case for functional contextualism in research on human behavior. *Applied and Preventive Psychology: Current Scientific Perspectives, 5,* 47-57.

Birx, E. (2002). *Healing Zen: Awakening to a Life of Wholeness and Compassion While Caring for Yourself and Others.* New York: Viking Compass.

Bishop, S. R., Lau, M., Shapiro, S., Carlson, L., Anderson, N. D., Carmody, J., & Devins, G. (2004). Mindfulness: A proposed operational definition. *Clinical Psychology: Science and Practice, 11*(3), 230-241.

Bohus, M., Haaf, B., Stiglmayer, C., Pohl, U., Bohme, R., & Linehan, M. (2000). Evaluation of inpatient dialectical-behavior therapy for borderline personality disorder: A prospective study. *Behaviour Research and Therapy, 38,* 875-887.

Bond, F. W., & Bunce, D. (2000). Mediators of change in emotion-focused and problem focused worksite stress management interventions. *Journal of Occupational Health Psychology, 5,* 156-163.

Bond, F. W., & Flaxman, P. E. (2006). The ability of psychological flexibility and job control to predict learning, job performance, and mental health. In S. C. Hayes, F. W. Bond, D. Barnes-Holmes, & J. Austin (Eds.),

Acceptance and Mindfulness at Work (pp. 113-130). New York: Haworth Press.

Bond, F. W., Hayes, S. C., & Barnes-Homes, D. (2006). Psychological flexibility, ACT, and organizational behavior. In S. C. Hayes, F. W. Bond, D. Barnes-Holmes, & J. Austin (Eds.). *Acceptance and Mindfulness at Work* (pp. 25-54). New York: The Haworth Press.

Bowen, S. (2008). *Effects of mindfulness-based instructions on negative affect, urges and smoking* (Doctoral dissertation, University of Washington, Publication No. AAT 3328375).

Bowen, S., Chawla, N., Collins, S., Witkiewitz, K., Hsu, S., Grow, J., . . . Marlatt, A. (2009). Mindfulness-based relapse prevention for substance use disorders: A pilot efficacy trial. *Substance Abuse, 30,* 295-305. DOI: 10.1080/08897070903250084

Bowen, S., Chawla, N., & Marlatt, G. A. (2010). *Mindfulness-Based Relapse Prevention for Addictive Behaviors: A Clinician's Guide.* New York: Guilford Press

Bowen, S., & Marlatt, A. (2009). Surfing the urge: Brief mindfulness-based intervention for college student smokers. *Psychology of Addictive Behaviors, 23*(4), 666-671.

Brach, T. (2003). *Radical Acceptance: Embracing Your Life With the Heart of a Buddha.* New York: Bantam Books.

Brazier, D. (1995). *Zen Therapy: Transcending the Sorrows of the Human Mind.* New York: John Wiley & Sons.

Brotto, L. A., Basson, R., & Luria M. A. (2008). Mindfulness-based group psychoeducational intervention targeting sexual arousal disorder in women. *Journal of Sexual Medicine, 5,* 1646-1659.

Brotto, L. A., & Heiman, J. R. (2007). Mindfulness in sex therapy: Applications for women with sexual difficulties following gynecologic cancer. *Sexual and Relationship Therapy, 22,* 3-11.

Brotto, L., Heiman, J., Goff, B., Greer, B., Lentz, G., Swisher, E., Tamimi, H., & Van Blaricom, A. (2008). A psychoeducational intervention for sexual dysfunction in women with gynecologic cancer. *Archives of Sexual Behavior, 37,* 317-329.

Brotto, L. A., Krychman, M., & Jacobson, P. (2008). Eastern approaches for enhancing women's sexuality: Mindfulness, acupuncture, and yoga. *Journal of Sexual Medicine, 5,* 2741-2748.

Burke, C. (2010). Mindfulness-based approaches with children and adolescents: A preliminary review of current research in an emergent field. *Journal of Child and Family Studies, 19,* 133-144.

Burpee, L. C., & Langer, E. J. (2005). Mindfulness and marital satisfaction. *Journal of Adult Development, 12*(1), 43-51.

Butler, A. C., Chapman, J. E., Forman, E. M., & Beck, A. T. (2006). The empirical status of cognitive-behavioral therapy: A review of meta-analyses. *Clinical Psychology Review, 26*(1), 17-31.

Cahn, B. R., & Polich, J. (2006). Meditation states and traits: EEG, ERP, and neuroimaging studies. *Psychological Bulletin, 132,* 180-211.

Carson, J. W., Carson, K. M., Gil, K. M., & Baucom, D. H. (2004). Mindfulness-based relationship enhancement. *Behavior Therapy, 35,* 471-494.

Center for Mindfulness. (n.d.). *Mindful Leadership Programs.* Retrieved from http://www.umassmed.edu/cfm/leadership/index.aspx

Chung, C. (1990). Psychotherapist and expansion of awareness. *Psychotherapy and Psychosomatics, 53,* 28-32.

Cleary, T. (1997). *Stopping and Seeing: A Comprehensive Course in Buddhist Meditation.* Boston: Shambhala Publications.

Coder, C. (2004). *Children and Grief: Training for Teachers* (Unpublished doctoral dissertation). Wright State University, Dayton, OH.

Covey, S. (2004). *The Seven Habits of Highly Effective People.* New York: Free Press.

Crane, R. (2009). *Mindfulness Based Cognitive Therapy.* London and New York: Routledge.

Critchley, H. D. (2005). Neural mechanisms of autonomic, affective and cognitive integration. *Journal of Comparative Neurology, 493,* 154-166.

Danna, K., & Griffin, R. (1999). Health and well-being in the workplace: A review and synthesis of the literature. *Journal of Management, 25*(3), 357-385.

D'Aquili, E. G., & Newberg, A. B. (1999). *The Mystical Mind: Probing the Biology of Religious Experience.* Minneapolis, MN: Fortress Press.

Denton, R. B., & Sears, R. W. (2009). The clinical uses of mindfulness. In J. B. Allen, E. M. Wolf, & L. VanderCreek (Eds.), *Innovations in Clinical Practice: A 21st Century Sourcebook* (Vol. 1, pp. 135-148). Sarasota, FL: Professional Resource Press.

Didonna, F. (2009a). Introduction: Where new and old paths to dealing with suffering meet. In F. Didonna (Ed.), *Clinical Handbook of Mindfulness* (pp. 1-14). New York: Springer.

Didonna, F. (2009b). Mindfulness-based interventions in an inpatient setting. In F. Didonna (Ed.), *Clinical Handbook of Mindfulness* (pp. 447-461). New York: Springer.

Dimeff, L. A., Koerner, K., & Linehan, M. M. (Eds.) (2007). *Dialectical Behavior Therapy in Clinical Practice: Applications Across Disorders and Settings.* New York: Guilford Press.

Duncan, L. G., & Bardacke, N. (2009). Mindfulness-based childbirth and parenting education: Promoting family mindfulness during the perinatal period. *Journal of Child & Family Studies, 19*, 190-202. doi 10.1007/s10826-009-9313-7.

Epstein, R. M. (1995). *Thoughts Without Thinker.* New York: Basic Books.

Epstein, R. M. (1998). *Going to Pieces Without Falling Apart: A Buddhist Perspective on Wholeness: Lessons From Meditation and Psychotherapy.* New York: Broadway Books.

Epstein, R. M. (2003a). Mindful practice in action (I): Technical competence, evidence-based medicine, and relationship centered care. *Families, Systems & Health, 21*(1), 1-9.

Epstein, R. M. (2003b). Mindful practice in action (II): Cultivating habits of mind. *Families, Systems & Health, 21*(1), 11-17.

Farb, N. A. S., Anderson, A. K., Mayberg, H., Bean, J., McKeon, D., & Segal, Z. V. (2010). Minding one's emotions: Mindfulness training alters the neural expression of sadness. *Emotion, 10*(1), 25-33.

Farb, N., Segal, Z., Mayberg, H., Bean, J., McKeon, D., & Anderson, A. (2007). Mindfulness training reveals dissociable neural modes of self-reference. *Social, Cognitive and Affective Neuroscience, 2*, 313-322.

Fitzgerald, C., & Berger, J. (2002). *Executive Coaching: Practices and Perspectives.* Palo Alto, CA: Davies-Black Publishing.

Flaherty, J. (1999). *Coaching: Provoking Excellence in Others.* Boston: Butterworth-Heinemann.

Flaxman, P. E., & Bond, F. W. (2006). Acceptance and commitment therapy in the workplace. In R. Baer (Ed.), *Mindfulness-Based Treatment Approaches: Clinician's Guide to Evidence Base and Applications* (pp. 377-402). Burlington, MA: Academic Press (Elsevier).

Fletcher, L., & Hayes, S. C. (2005). Relational Frame Theory, Acceptance and Commitment Therapy, and a functional analytic definition of mindfulness. *Journal of Rational-Emotive and Cognitive-Behavioral Therapy, 23*(4), 315-336.

Florian, V., & Mikulincer, M. (2004). A multifaceted perspective on the existential meanings, manifestations, and consequences of the fear of personal death. In J. Greenberg, S. Koole, & T. Pyszczynski (Eds.), *Handbook of Experimental Existential Psychology* (pp. 54-70). New York: Guilford Press.

Forman, E. M., Herbert, P. D., Moitra, E. M., Yoemans, P. D., & Geller, P. A. (2007). A randomized controlled effectiveness trial of Acceptance and Commitment Therapy and Cognitive Therapy for anxiety and depression. *Behavior Modification, 31*, 772-799.

Fouad, N., Gerstein, L., & Toporek, R. (2006). Social justice and counseling psychology in context. In R. Toporek, L. Gerstein, N. Fouad, G. Roysircar, & T. Israel (Eds.), *Handbook for Social Justice in Counseling Psychology* (pp. 1-16). Thousand Oaks, CA: Sage Publications.

Freud, S. (1963). *Civilizations and Its Discontents*. London: Hogarth Press.

Fromm, E., Suzuki, D. T., & DeMartino, R. (1960). *Zen Buddhism and Psychoanalysis*. New York: Harper.

Fruzzetti, A. E. (2006). *The High Conflict Couple: A Dialectical Behavior Therapy Guide to Finding Peace, Intimacy, & Validation*. Oakland, CA: New Harbinger Publications.

Fruzzetti, A. E., Santisteban, D. A., & Hoffman, P. D. (2007). Dialectical behavior therapy with families. In L. A. Dimeff, K. Koerner, & M. M. Linehan (Eds.), *Dialectical Behavior Therapy in Clinical Practice: Applications Across Disorders and Settings* (pp. 222-244). New York: Guilford Press.

Fulton, P. R. (2005). Mindfulness as clinical training. In C. K. Germer, R. D. Siegel, & P. R. Fulton (Eds.), *Mindfulness and Psychotherapy* (pp. 55-72). New York: Guilford Press.

Gaudiano, B., & Herbert, J. (2006). Acute treatment of inpatients with psychotic symptoms using Acceptance and Commitment Therapy: Pilot results. *Behaviour Research and Therapy, 44*(3), 415-437.

Germer, C. K. (2005). Mindfulness: What is it? What does it matter? In C. K. Germer, R. D. Siegel, & P. R. Fulton (Eds.), *Mindfulness and Psychotherapy* (pp. 3-27). New York: Guilford Press.

Germer, C. K. (2009). *The Mindful Path to Self-Compassion: Freeing Yourself From Destructive Thoughts and Emotions*. New York: Guilford Press.

Gilbert, P. (Ed.). (2005). *Compassion: Conceptualisations, Research and Use in Psychotherapy*. New York: Routledge.

Gilbert, P. (2007). Evolved minds and compassion in the therapeutic relationship. In P. Gilbert & R. Leahy (Eds.), *The Therapeutic Relationship in the Cognitive Behavioral Psychotherapies*. New York: Routledge.

Gilbert, P. (2009). *The Compassionate Mind*. London: Constable.

Gilbert, P., & Irons, C. (2005). Focused therapies and compassionate mind training for shame and self-attacking. In P. Gilbert (Ed.), *Compassion: Conceptualisations, Research and Use in Psychotherapy* (pp. 263-326). New York: Routledge.

Gilbert, P., & Procter, S. (2006). Compassionate mind training for people with high shame and self-criticism: A pilot study of a group therapy approach. *Clinical Psychology and Psychotherapy, 13*, 353-379.

Goldin, P. R., & Gross, J. J. (2010). Effects of mindfulness-based stress reduction (MBSR) on emotional regulation in social anxiety disorder. *Emotion, 10*(1), 83-91.

Goleman, D., & Kabat-Zinn, J. (2007). *Mindfulness @ Work* [Audio CD]. New York: MacMillan Audio.

Gordon, J., & Johnson, M. (2003). Race, speech, and hostile educational environment: What color is free speech? *Journal of Social Philosophy, 34*, 414-436.

Gratz, K. L., Tull, M. T., & Wagner, A. W. (2005). Applying DBT mindfulness skills to the treatment of clients with anxiety disorders. In S. M. Orsillo & L. Roemer (Eds.), *Acceptance and Mindfulness-Based Approaches to Anxiety Conceptualization and Treatment*. New York: Springer.

Grossman, P., Niemann, L., Schmidt, S., & Walach, H. (2004). Mindfulness-based stress reduction and health benefits: A meta-analysis. *Journal of Psychosomatic Research, 57,* 35-43.

Guthrie, R. V. (2003). *Even the Rat Was White: A Historical View of Psychology* (2ⁿᵈ ed.). Boston: Allyn & Bacon.

Haaga, D. A. F., Dyck, M. J., & Ernst, D. (1991). Empirical status of cognitive theory of depression. *Psychological Bulletin, 110,* 215-236.

Haas, J. R., & Hayes, S. C. (2006). When knowing you are doing well hinders performance: Exploring the interaction between rules and feedback. In S. C. Hayes, F. W. Bond, D. Barnes-Holmes, & J. Austin (Eds.), *Acceptance and Mindfulness at Work* (pp. 91-112). New York: Haworth Press.

Hanh, T. N. (1975). *The Miracle of Mindfulness*. Boston, MA: Beacon Press.

Hanh, T. N. (2001). *Anger: Wisdom for Cooling the Flames*. New York: Riverhead Books.

Hargrove, R. (1995). *Masterful Coaching*. San Diego, CA: Pfeiffer.

Hargrove, R., & Kaestner, C. (1998). *Masterful Coaching Field Guide*. San Diego, CA: Pfeiffer.

Harris, R. (2007). *The Happiness Trap*. Boston: Trumpeter.

Harris, R. (2009, October). Mindfulness without meditation. *Healthcare Counselling and Psychotherapy Journal,* pp. 21-24.

Harvey, P., & Penzo, J. (2009). *Parenting a Child Who Has Intense Emotions: Dialectical Behavior Therapy Skills to Help Your Child Regulate Emotional Outbursts and Aggressive Behaviors*. Oakland, CA: New Harbinger Publications.

Hayes, S. C. (2004). Acceptance and Commitment Therapy and the new behavior therapies: Mindfulness, acceptance, and relationship. In S. C. Hayes, V. M. Follete, & M. M. Linehan (Eds.), *Mindfulness and Acceptance* (pp. 1-29). New York: Guilford Press.

Hayes, S. C. (2007). Commentary: Language, self, and diversity. In J. C. Muran (Ed.), *Dialogues on Difference: Studies of Diversity in the Therapeutic Relationship* (pp. 275-279). Washington, DC: American Psychological Association. doi: 10.1037/11500-030

Hayes, S. C. (2008). *Acceptance & Commitment Therapy (ACT): Helping Your Clients Get Out of Their Minds and Into Their Lives* [Audio CD]. Eau Claire, WI: PESI, LLC.

Hayes, S. C., Barnes-Holmes, D., & Roche, B. (Eds.). (2001). *Relational Frame Theory: A Post-Skinnerian Account of Human Language and Cognition*. New York: Plenum Press.

Hayes, S. C., Bunting, K., Herbst, S., Bond, F. W., & Barnes-Holmes, D. (2006). Expanding the scope of organizational behavior management: Relational frame theory and the experimental analysis of complex human behavior. In S. C. Hayes, F. W. Bond, D. Barnes-Holmes, & J. Austin (Eds.), *Acceptance and Mindfulness at Work* (pp. 1-24). New York: Haworth Press.

Hayes, S. C., Luoma, J., Bond, F., Masuda, A., & Lillis, J. (2006). Acceptance and Commitment Therapy: Model, processes, and outcomes. *Behaviour Research and Therapy, 44*(1), 1-25.

Hayes, S. C., & Smith, S. (2005). *Get Out of Your Mind and Into Your Life.* Oakland, CA: New Harbinger Publications.

Hayes, S. C., Strosahl, K. D., & Wilson, K. G. (1999). *Acceptance and Commitment Therapy: An Experiential Approach to Behavior Change.* New York: Guilford Press.

Hayes, S. C., Strosahl, K. D., Wilson, K. G., Bissett, R. T., Pistorello, J., Toarmino, D., . . . McCurry, S. M. (2004). Measuring experiential avoidance: A preliminary test of a working model. *The Psychological Record, 54,* 553-578.

Hayes, S. C., Wilson, K. W., Gifford, E. V., Follette, V. M., & Strosahl, K. (1996). Experiential avoidance and behavioral disorders: A functional dimensional approach to diagnosis and treatment. *Journal of Consulting and Clinical Psychology, 64*(6), 1152-1168.

Hayes, S. K. (1993). *Action Meditation: The Japanese Diamond and Lotus Tradition.* Dayton, OH: SKH Quest Center.

Hayes, S. K. (2000). *How to Own the World: A Guide for Taking the Path of the Spiritual Explorer.* Dayton, OH: SKH Quest Center.

Heiman, J., & LoPiccolo J. (1987). *Becoming Orgasmic: A Sexual and Personal Growth Program for Women.* New York: Fireside.

Helms, J. E. (1992). *A Race is a Nice Thing to Have: A Guide to Being a White Person or Understanding the White Persons in Your Life.* Topeka, KS: Content Communications.

Hirai, T. (1989). *Zen Meditation and Psychotherapy.* New York: Japan Publications.

Hofmann, S., Sawyer, A., Witt, A., & Oh, D. (2010). The effect of mindfulness-based therapy on anxiety and depression: A meta-analytic review. *Journal of Consulting and Clinical Psychology, 78*(10), 169-183.

Hollon, S. D., & Beck, A. T. (1986). Cognitive and cognitive-behavioral therapies. In A. E. Bergin & S. L. Garfield (Eds.), *Handbook of Psychotherapy and Behavior Change* (3rd ed., pp. 446-448). New York: Wiley.

Honarparvaran, N., Tabrizy, M., Navabinejad, Sh., Shafiabady, A., & Moradi, M. (2010). The efficacy of acceptance and commitment therapy (ACT) training with regard to reducing sexual dissatisfaction among couples. *European Journal of Social Sciences, 15*(1), 166-172.

Hooker, K. E., & Fodor, I. E. (2008). Teaching mindfulness to children. *Gestalt Review, 12*(1), 75-91.

Ingram, R. E., & Hollon, S. D. (1986). Cognitive therapy for depression from an information processing perspective. In R. E. Ingram (Ed.), *Information Processing Approaches to Clinical Psychology* (pp. 259-281). Orlando, FL: Academic Press.

Jacobson, E. (1938). *Progressive Relaxation*. Chicago: University of Chicago Press.

Kabat-Zinn, J. (1982). An outpatient program in behavioral medicine for chronic pain patients based on the practice of mindfulness meditation: Theoretical considerations and preliminary results. *General Hospital Psychiatry, 4,* 33-47.

Kabat-Zinn, J. (1990). *Full Catastrophe Living: Using the Wisdom of Your Body and Mind to Face Stress, Pain, and Illness.* New York: Dell.

Kabat-Zinn, J. (1994). *Wherever You Go There You Are.* New York: Hyperion.

Kabat-Zinn, J. (2003). Mindfulness-based interventions in context: Past, present, and future. *Clinical Psychology: Science and Practice, 10*(2), 144-156.

Kabat-Zinn, J. (2009). Foreword. In F. Didonna (Ed.), *Clinical Handbook of Mindfulness* (pp. xxv-xxxii). New York: Springer.

Kabat-Zinn, J., Lipworth, L., Burney, R., & Sellers, W. (1985). The clinical use of mindfulness meditation for the self-regulation of chronic pain. *Journal of Behavioral Medicine, 8,* 163-190.

Kabat-Zinn, J., Lipworth, L., Burney, R., & Sellers, W. (1986). Four year follow-up of a meditation-based program for self-regulation of chronic pain: Treatment outcomes and compliance. *Clinical Journal of Pain, 2,* 159-173.

Kabat-Zinn, J., Massion, A. O., Kristeller, J., Peterson, L. G., Fletcher, K. E., Pbert, L., Lenderking, W. R., & Santorelli, S. (1992). Effectiveness of a meditation based stress reduction program in the treatment of anxiety disorders. *American Journal of Psychiatry, 149*, 936-943.

Kabat-Zinn, M., & Kabat-Zinn, J. (1997). *Everyday Blessings: The Inner Work of Mindful Parenting.* New York: Hyperion.

Kapleau, P. (1989). *The Wheel of Life and Death: A Practical and Spiritual Guide.* New York: Doubleday.

Kelly, A. C., Zuroff, D. C., Foa, C. L., & Gilbert, P. (2010). Who benefits from training in self-compassionate self-regulation? A study of smoking reduction. *Journal of Social and Clinical Psychology, 29*(7), 727-755.

Kieviet-Stijnen, A., Visser, A., Garssen, B., & Hudig, W. (2008). Mindfulness-based stress reduction training for oncology patients: Patients' appraisal and changes in well-being. *Patient Education and Counseling, 72*, 436-442.

Kilburg, R. R. (2000). *Executive Coaching: Developing Managerial Wisdom in a World of Chaos*. Washington, DC: American Psychological Association.

Koons, C. R., Robins, C. J., Tweed, J. L., Lynch, T. R., Gonzalez, A. M., Morse, . . . Bastian, L. A. (2001). Efficacy of dialectical behavior therapy in women veterans with borderline personality disorder. *Behavior Therapy, 32,* 371-390.

Kristeller, J. L. (2003) Mindfulness, wisdom and eating: Applying a multi-domain model of meditation effects. *Journal of Constructivism in the Human Sciences, 8,* 107-118.

Kristeller, J. L., Baer, R. A., & Quillian-Wolever, R. W. (2006). Mindfulness-based approaches to eating disorders. In R. A. Baer (Ed.), *Mindfulness and Acceptance-Based Interventions: Conceptualization, Application, and Empirical Support* (pp. 75-91). San Diego, CA: Elsevier.

Kristeller, J. L., & Hallett, C. B. (1999). An exploratory study of a meditation-based intervention for binge eating disorder. *Journal of Health Psychology, 4,* 357-363.

Kubler-Ross, E. (1997). *On Death and Dying*. New York: Scribner Classics.

Lazar, S. W., Kerr, C. E., Wasserman, R. H., Gray, J. R., Greve, D. N., Treadway, M. T., . . . Fischl, B. (2005). Meditation experience is associated with increased cortical thickness. *Neuroreport, 16*(17), 1893-1897.

Lee, J., Semple, R. J., Rosa, D., & Miller, L. (2008). Mindfulness-based cognitive therapy for children: Results of a pilot study. *Journal of Cognitive Psychotherapy: An International Quarterly, 22*(1), 15-28.

Lengacher, C., Johnson-Mallard, V., Post-White, J., Moscoso, M., Jacobsen, P., Klein, T., . . . Kip, K. (2009). Randomized controlled trial of mindfulness-based stress reduction (MBSR) for survivors of breast cancer. *Psycho-Oncology, 18,* 1261-1272.

Lesh, T. V. (1970). Zen meditation and the development of empathy in counselors. *Journal of Humanistic Psychology, 10,* 39-74.

Linehan, M. M. (1993a). *Cognitive-Behavioral Therapy for Borderline Personality Disorder*. New York: Guilford Press.

Linehan, M. M. (1993b). *Skills Training Manual for Treating Borderline Personality Disorder*. New York: Guilford Press.

Linehan, M. M. (1997). Validation and psychotherapy. In L. Greenberg (Ed.), *Empathy Reconsidered: New Directions in Psychotherapy* (pp. 353-392). Washington, DC: American Psychological Association.

Linehan, M. M. (2005). *From Suffering to Freedom: Practicing Reality Acceptance* (from the Chaos to Freedom DVD Series). New York: Guilford.

Linehan, M. M., Armstrong, H. E., Suarez, A., Allmon, D., & Heard, H. L. (1991). Cognitive-behavioral treatment of chronically parasuicidal borderline patients. *Archives of General Psychiatry, 48,* 1060-1064.

Linehan, M. M., Comtois, K. A., Murray, A. M., Brown, M. Z., Gallop, R. J., . . . Lindenboim, N. (2006). Two-year randomized controlled trial and follow-up of Dialectical Behavior Therapy vs. therapy by experts for suicidal behaviors and Borderline Personality Disorder. *Archives of General Psychiatry, 63*, 757-766.

Linehan, M. M., Heard, H. L., & Armstrong, H. E. (1993). Naturalistic follow-up of a behavioral treatment for chronically parasuicidal borderline patients. *Archives of General Psychiatry, 50*, 971-974.

Linehan, M. M., Schmidt, H., Dimeff, L. A., Kanter, J. W., Craft, J. C., Comtois, K. A., & Recknor, K. L. (1999). Dialectical Behavior Therapy for patients with Borderline Personality Disorder and drug-dependence. *American Journal on Addiction, 8*, 279-292.

Longmore, R. J., & Worrell, M. (2007). Do we need to challenge thoughts in cognitive behavior therapy? *Clinical Psychology Review, 27*, 173-187.

Luoma, J. B., Hayes, S. C., & Walser, R. (2007). *Learning ACT: An Acceptance & Commitment Therapy Skills-Training Manual for Therapists.* Oakland, CA: New Harbinger, & Reno, NV: Context Press.

Lush, E., Salmon, P., Floyd, A., Studts, J., Weissbecker, I., & Sephton, S. (2009). Mindfulness meditation for symptom reduction in fibromyalgia: Psychophysiological correlates. *Journal of Clinical Psychology in Medical Settings, 16*(2), 200-207. doi: 10.1007/s10880-009-9153-z.

Lynch, P. (2006). *Five Mountain Record: The Kôan Collection of the Five Mountain Order.* Long Beach, CA: Before Thought Publications.

Lynch, T. R., & Cheavens, J. S. (2007). Dialectical behavior therapy for depression and comorbid personality disorder: An extension of standard dialectical behavior therapy with a special emphasis on the treatment of older adults. In L. A. Dimeff, K. Koerner, & M. M. Linehan (Eds.), *Dialectical Behavior Therapy in Clinical Practice: Applications Across Disorders and Settings.* New York: Guilford Press.

Ma, S. H., & Teasdale, J. D. (2004). Mindfulness-based cognitive therapy for depression: Replication and exploration of differential relapse prevention effects. *Journal of Consulting and Clinical Psychology, 72*, 31-40.

Mahesh Yogi, M. (1995). *Science of Being and Art of Living: Transcendental Meditation.* New York: Penguin Books USA.

Marlatt, G. A. (2010). *Mindfulness and Recovery From Addiction.* Retrieved from http://www.uwpsychiatry.org/Media/Marlatt_GR_Slides.pdf

Marlatt, G. A., & Gordon, J. R. (1985). *Relapse Prevention: Maintenance Strategies in the Treatment of Addictive Behaviors.* New York: Guilford.

Marra, T. (2004). *Depressed and Anxious: The Dialectical Behavior Therapy Workbook for Overcoming Depression & Anxiety.* Oakland, CA: New Harbinger Publications.

Martin, J. (1997). Mindfulness: A proposed common factor. *Journal of Psychotherapy Integration, 7*(4), 291-312.

Martin, P. (1999). *The Zen Path Through Depression.* New York: HarperCollins Publishers.

McBee, L. (2008). *Mindfulness-Based Elder Care: A CAM Model for Frail Elders and Their Caregivers.* New York: Springer.

McBee, L. (2009). Mindfulness-based elder care: Communicating mindfulness to frail elders and their caregivers. In F. Didonna (Ed.), *Clinical Handbook of Mindfulness* (pp. 431-445). New York: Springer.

McBee, L., Westreich, L., & Likourezos, A. (2004). A psychoeducational relaxation group for pain and stress management in the nursing home. *Journal of Social Work in Long-Term Care, 3*(1), 15-28.

McCann, R. A., Ivanoff, A., Schmidt, H., & Beach, B. (2007). Implementing dialectical behavior therapy in residential forensic settings with adults and juveniles. In L. A. Dimeff, K. Koerner, & M. M. Linehan (Eds.), *Dialectical Behavior Therapy in Clinical Practice: Applications Across Disorders and Settings* (pp. 112-144). New York: Guilford Press.

McDonald, K., & Courtin, R. (2005). *How to Meditate: A Practical Guide* (2nd ed.). Boston: Wisdom Publications.

McMain, S., Sayrs, J. H. R., Dimeff, L. A., & Linehan, M. M. (2007). Dialectical behavior therapy for individuals with borderline personality disorder and substance dependence. In L. A. Dimeff, K. Koerner, & M. M. Linehan (Eds.), *Dialectical Behavior Therapy in Clinical Practice: Applications Across Disorders and Settings* (pp. 145-173). New York: Guilford Press.

Miller, A. L., Rathus, J. H., DuBose, A. P., Dexter-Mazza, E. T., & Goldklang, A. R. (2007). Dialectical behavior therapy for adolescents. In L. A. Dimeff, K. Koerner, & M. M. Linehan (Eds.), *Dialectical Behavior Therapy in Clinical Practice: Applications Across Disorders and Settings* (pp. 245-263). New York: Guilford Press.

Miller, A. L., Rathus, J. H., & Linehan, M. M. (2006). *Dialectical Behavior Therapy With Suicidal Adolescents.* New York: Guilford Press.

Miller, J., & Brown, P. (1993). *The Corporate Coach: How to Build a Team of Loyal Customers and Happy Employees.* New York: HarperBusiness.

Miller, J. J., Fletcher, K., & Kabat-Zinn, J. (1995). Three-year follow-up and clinical implications of a mindfulness meditation-based stress reduction intervention in the treatment of anxiety disorders. *General Hospital Psychiatry, 17,* 192-200.

Mingyur, Y. (2007). *The Joy of Living: Unlocking the Secret and Science of Happiness.* New York: Harmony Books.

Napoli, M., Krech, P. K., & Holley, L. C. (2005). Mindfulness training for elementary school students: The attention academy. *Journal of Applied School Psychology, 2*(1), 99-125.

Newberg, A., D'Aquili, E., & Rause, V. (2001). *Why God Won't Go Away: Brain Science and the Biology of Belief.* New York: Random House.

Niebuhr, R. (ca. 1937-1943). *Serenity Prayer* [appeared in various forms in unpublished or private settings and later adopted by Alcoholics Anonymous].

Nolen-Hoeksema, S. (2000). The role of rumination in depressive disorders and mixed anxiety/depressive symptoms. *Journal of Abnormal Psychology, 109,* 504-511.

Ogden, C. L., Carroll, M. D., Curtin, L. R., McDowell, M. A., Tabak, C. J., & Flegal, K. M. (2006). Prevalence of overweight and obesity in the United States, 1999-2004. *The Journal of the American Medical Association, 295,* 1549-1555.

O'Hora, D., & Maglieri, K. A. (2006). Goal statements and goal-directed behavior: A relational frame account of goal setting in organizations. In S. C. Hayes, F. W. Bond, D. Barnes-Holmes, & J. Austin (Eds.). *Acceptance and Mindfulness at Work* (pp. 131-170). New York: Haworth Press.

Orsillo, S. M., Roemer, L., Lerner, J. B., & Tull, M. (2004). Acceptance, mindfulness, and cognitive-behavioral therapy: Comparisons, contrasts, and application to anxiety. In S. C. Hayes, V. M. Follete, & M. M. Linehan (Eds.), *Mindfulness and Acceptance* (pp. 66-95). New York: Guilford Press.

Pawle, R. (2008, January). *Koans and Attention: The Use of Zen Buddhist Practices in Psychotherapy.* Paper presented at the World Congress on Psychology and Spirituality in Delhi, India.

Posner, M. I., & Rafal, R. D. (1986). Cognitive theories of attention and the rehabilitation of attentional deficits. In M. J. Meier, A. L. Benton, & L. Miller (Eds.), *Neuropsychological Rehabilitation* (pp. 182-201). New York: Guilford Press.

Prochaska, J. O., & DiClemente, C. C. (1992). Stages of change in the modification of problem behaviors. *Progress in Behavior Modification, 28,* 183-218.

Reynolds, S. K., Wolbert, R., Abney-Cunningham, G., & Patterson, K. (2007). Dialectical behavior therapy for assertive community treatment teams. In L. A. Dimeff, K. Koerner, & M. M. Linehan (Eds.), *Dialectical Behavior Therapy in Clinical Practice: Applications Across Disorders and Settings* (pp. 298-325). New York: Guilford Press.

Rinpoche, Y. M. (2007). *The Joy of Living: Unlocking the Secret & Science of Happiness.* New York: Crown Publishing.

Rinpoche, S. (2002). *The Tibetan Book of Living and Dying: Revised and Updated.* San Francisco: Harper San Francisco.

Rizvi, S. L., Monroe-DeVita, M., & Dimeff, L. A. (2007). Evaluating your dialectical behavior therapy program. In L. A. Dimeff, K. Koerner, & M. M. Linehan (Eds.), *Dialectical Behavior Therapy in Clinical Practice: Applications Across Disorders and Settings* (pp. 326-350). New York: Guilford Press.

Rizvi, S. L., Welch, S. S., & Dimidjian, S. (2009). Mindfulness and borderline personality disorder. In F. Didonna (Ed.), *Clinical Handbook of Mindfulness* (pp. 245-258). New York: Springer.

Roemer, L., & Orsillo, S. M. (2009). *Mindfulness & Acceptance-Based Behavioral Therapies in Practice*. New York: Guilford Press.

Rollnick, S. (2009). *Motivational Interviewing for Mental Health Disorders*. Audio CD from PESI, Inc.

Rosenbaum, R. (1999). *Zen and the Heart of Psychotherapy*. Philadelphia, PA: Taylor & Francis.

Rosenzweig, S., Greeson, J. M., Reibel, D. K., Green, J. S., Jasser, S. A., & Beasley, D. (2010). Mindfulness-based stress reduction for chronic pain conditions: Variation in treatment outcomes and role of home meditation practice. *Journal of Psychosomatic Research, 68*(1), 29-36.

Rosenzweig, S., Reibel, D. K., Greeson, J. M., Edman, J. S., Jasser, S. A., McMearty, K. D., & Goldstein, B. J. (2007). Mindfulness-based stress reduction is associated with improved glycemic control in type 2 diabetes mellitus: A pilot study. *Alternative Therapies, 13*(5), 36-38.

Safer, D. L., Telch, C. F., & Chen, E. Y. (2009). *Dialectical Behavior Therapy for Binge Eating and Bulimia*. New York: Guilford Press.

Safran, J. D., Muran, J. C., Stevens, C., & Rothman, M. (2008). A relational approach to supervision: Addressing ruptures in the alliance. In C. A. Falender & E. P. Shafranske (Eds.), *Casebook for Clinical Supervision: A Competency-Based Approach*. Washington, DC: American Psychological Association.

Safran, J. D., & Segal, Z. V. (1990). *Interpersonal Process in Cognitive Therapy*. New York: Basic Books.

Sahn, S. (1997). *The Compass of Zen*. Boston, MA: Shambhala Publications.

Saltzman, A., & Goldin, P. (2008). Mindfulness-based stress reduction for school-age children. In S. C. Hayes & L. E. Greco (Eds.), *Acceptance and Mindfulness Treatments for Children & Adolescents: A Practicioner's Guide*. Oakland, CA: New Harbinger Publications.

Salzberg, S. (1995). *Loving-kindness: The Revolutionary Art of Happiness*. Boston: Shambhala Publications.

Schneider, K. J. (2003). Existential-humanistic psychotherapies. In A. S. Gurman & S. B. Messer (Eds.), *Essential Psychotherapies: Theory and Practice* (2nd ed., pp. 149-181). New York: Guilford Press.

Schuster, R. (1979). Empathy and mindfulness. *Journal of Humanistic Psychology, 19*(1), 71-77.

Sears, R. (2009). Mindfulness in clinical practice: A basic overview. *Ohio Psychologist, 56*, August.

Sears, R., Rudisill, J., & Mason-Sears, C. (2006). *Consultation Skills for Mental Health Professionals*. New York: John Wiley & Sons.

Segal, Z. V. (2008). *Mindfulness-based Cognitive Therapy for Depression and Anxiety* [CD]. Lancaster, PA: J&K Seminars, LLC.

Segal, Z. V., Teasdale, J. D., & Williams, J. M. (2004). Mindfulness-Based cognitive therapy: Theoretical rationale and empirical status. In S. C. Hayes, V. M. Follete, & M. M. Linehan (Eds.), *Mindfulness and Acceptance* (pp. 45-65). New York: Guilford Press.

Segal, Z. V., Williams, J. M. G., & Teasdale, J. D. (2002). *Mindfulness-based Cognitive Therapy for Depression: A New Approach to Preventing Relapse*. New York: Guilford.

Segal, Z. V., Williams, J. M. G., Teasdale, J. D., & Gemar M. (1996). A cognitive science perspective on kindling and episode sensitization in recurrent affective disorder. *Psychological Medicine, 26,* 371-380.

Semple, R. J., & Lee, J. (2011). *Mindfulness-Based Cognitive Therapy for Anxious Children: A Manual for Treating Childhood Anxiety*. Oakland, CA: New Harbinger.

Semple, R. J., Lee, J., Rosa, D., & Miller, L. F. (2010). A randomized trial of mindfulness-based cognitive therapy for children: Promoting mindful attention to enhance social-emotional resiliency in children. *Journal of Child and Family Studies 19,* 218-229.

Semple, R. J., Reid, E. F. G., & Miller, L. (2005). Treating anxiety with mindfulness: An open trial of mindfulness training for anxious children. *Journal of Cognitive Psychotherapy: An International Quarterly, 19*(4), 379-392.

Senge, P. M., Scharmer, C. O., Jaworski, J., & Flowers, B. S. (2004). *Presence: Human Purpose and the Field of the Future*. Cambridge, MA: Society for Organizational Learning.

Sephton, S. E., Salmon, P., Weissbecker, I., Ulmer, C., Floyd, A., Hoover, K., & Studts, J. L. (2007). Mindfulness meditation alleviates depressive symptoms in women with fibromyalgia: Results of a randomized clinical trial. *Arthritis Care & Research, 57*(1), 77-85.

Shapiro, S., Astin, J., Bishop, S., & Cordova, M. (2005). Mindfulness-Based Stress Reduction for health care professionals: Results from a randomized trial. *International Journal of Stress Management, 12*(2), 164-176. doi:10.1037/1072-5245.12.2.164.

Shapiro, S. L., Bootzin, R. R., Figueredo, A. J., Lopez, A. M., & Schwartz, G. E. (2003). The efficacy of mindfulness-based stress reduction in the treatment of sleep disturbance in women with breast cancer: An exploratory study. *Journal of Psychosomatic Research, 54,* 85-91.

Shapiro, S. L., Schwartz, G. E., & Bonner, G. (1998). Effects of mindfulness-based stress reduction on medical and premedical students. *Journal of Behavioral Medicine, 21*(6), 581-599.

Siegel, D. J. (2007). *The Mindful Brain: Reflection and Attunement in the Cultivation of Well-being*. New York: W. W. Norton & Company.

Sneed, J. R., Balestri, M., & Belfi, B. (2003). The use of dialectical behavior therapy strategies in the psychiatric emergency room. *Psychotherapy: Theory, Research, Practice, Training, 40*(4), 265-277.

Society of Clinical Psychology [APA Division 12]. (no date). Retrieved from http://www.div12.org/psychologicaltreatments.bpd_dbt.html

Sohlberg, M. M., & Mateer, C. A. (1989). *Introduction to Cognitive Rehabilitation: Theory and Practice.* New York: Guilford Press.

Stewart, I., Barnes-Holmes, D., Barnes-Holmes, Y., Bond, F. W., & Hayes, S. C. (2006). Relational frame theory and industrial/organizational psychology. In S. C. Hayes, F. W. Bond, D. Barnes-Holmes, & J. Austin (Eds.), *Acceptance and Mindfulness at Work* (pp. 55-90). New York: Haworth Press.

Sue, D. W. (2003). *Overcoming Our Racism: The Journey to Liberation.* San Francisco: Jossey-Bass.

Sue, D. W., Capodilupo, C. M., Torino, G. C., Bucceri, J. M., Holder, A. M. B., Nadal, K. L., & Esquilin, M. (2007). Racial microaggressions in everyday life: Implications for clinical practice. *American Psychologist, 62*(4), 271-286. doi: 10.1037/0003-066X.62.4.271

Suzuki, S. (2006). *Zen Mind, Beginner's Mind.* Boston: Shambhala Publications.

Swenson, C. R., Witterholt, S., & Bohus, M. (2007). Dialectical behavior therapy on inpatient units. In L. A. Dimeff, K. Koerner, & M. M. Linehan (Eds.), *Dialectical Behavior Therapy in Clinical Practice: Applications Across Disorders and Settings* (pp. 69-110). New York: Guilford Press.

Tart, C. (1990). Extending mindfulness to everyday life. *Journal of Humanistic Psychology, 30*(1), 81-106.

Teasdale, J. D. (1988). Cognitive vulnerability to persistent depression. *Cognition and Emotion, 2,* 247-274.

Teasdale, J. D. (1997). The relationship between cognition and emotion: The mind-in-place in mood disorders. In D. M. Clark & C. G. Fairburn (Eds.), *The Science and Practice of Cognitive Behaviour Therapy* (pp. 67-93). New York: Oxford University Press.

Teasdale, J. D., Segal Z. V., & Williams, J. M. G., (1995). How does cognitive therapy prevent depressive relapse and why should attentional control (mindfulness) training help? *Behavioral Research and Therapy, 33,* 25-39.

Teasdale, J. D., Segal, Z. V., Williams, J. M. G., Ridgeway, V., Soulsby, J., & Lau, M. (2000). Prevention of relapse/recurrence in major depression by mindfulness-based cognitive therapy. *Journal of Consulting and Clinical Psychology, 68,* 615-623.

Thondup, T. (2008). *The Healing Power of Loving-kindness: A Guided Buddhist Meditation.* Boston: Shambhala Publications.

Ting-Toomey, S. (2009). A mindful approach to managing conflict in intercultural intimate couples. In T. A. Karis & K. D. Killian (Eds.), *Intercultural Couples: Exploring Diversity in Intimate Relationships* (pp. 31-49). New York: Routledge/Taylor & Francis Group.

Tirch, D. D. (2010). Mindfulness as a context for the cultivation of compassion. *International Journal of Cognitive Therapy, 3*(2), 113-123.

Tolkien, J. R. R. (1994). *The Lord of the Rings.* Boston: Houghton Mifflin Company.

Twemlow, S. W. (2001). Training psychotherapists in attributes of "mind" from Zen and psychoanalytic perspectives, Part I: Core principles, emptiness, impermanence, and paradox. *American Journal of Psychotherapy, 55*(1), 1-39.

Vacarr, B. (2001). Moving beyond polite correctness: Practicing mindfulness in the diverse classroom. *Harvard Educational Review, 71*(2), 285-295.

Van Dam, N. T., Sheppard, S. C., Forsyth, J. P., & Earleywine, M. (2011). Self-compassion is a better predictor than mindfulness of symptom severity and quality of life in mixed anxiety and depression. *Journal of Anxiety Disorders, 25*, 123-130.

Vanderploeg, R. D. (2000). *Clinician's Guide to Neuropsychological Assessment* (2nd ed.). Hillsdale, NJ: Lawrence Erlbaum.

Van Dijk, S. (2009). *The Dialectical Behavior Therapy Skills Workbook for Bipolar Disorder: Using DBT to Regain Control of Your Emotions and Your Life.* Oakland, CA: New Harbinger Publications.

Verheul, R., van den Bosch, L. M. C., Koeter, M. W. J., de Ridder, M. A. J., Stijnen, T., & van den Brink, W. (2003). A 12-month randomized clinical trial of Dialectical Behavior Therapy for women with borderline personality disorder in the Netherlands. *British Journal of Psychiatry, 182*, 135-140.

Vieten, C., & Astin, J. (2008). Effects of a mindfulness-based intervention during pregnancy on prenatal stress and mood: Results of a pilot study. *Women's Mental Health, 11*, 67-74.

Wachs, K., & Cordova, J. V. (2007). Mindful relating: Exploring mindfulness and emotion repertoires in intimate relationships. *Journal of Marital and Family Therapy, 33*(4), 464-481.

Wang, S. (2005). A conceptual framework for integrating research related to the physiology of compassion and the wisdom of Buddhist teachings. In P. Gilbert (Ed.), *Compassion: Conceptualisations, Research and Use in Psychotherapy* (pp. 75-120). New York: Routledge.

Watts, A. (1957). *The Way of Zen.* New York: Vintage Books.

Watts, A. (1961). *Psychotherapy East and West.* New York: Random House.

Watts, A. (2004). *Out of Your Mind: Essential Listening From the Alan Watts Audio Archives* [Audio CD]. Louisville, CO: Sounds True.

Wegner, D. M., Schneider, D. J., Carter, S., & White, T. (1987). Paradoxical effects of thought suppression. *Journal of Personality and Social Psychology, 53*, 5-13.

Weissbecker, I., Salmon, P., Studts, J. L., Floyd, A. R., Dedert, E. A., Sephton, S. E. (2002). Mindfulness-based stress reduction and sense of coherence among women with fibromyalgia. *Journal of Clinical Psychology in Medical Settings, 9*(4), 297-307.

Wenzlaff, R. M., & Wegner, D. M. (2000). Thought suppression. In S. T. Fiske (Ed.), *Annual Review of Psychology* (Vol. 51, pp. 59-91). Palo Alto, CA: Annual Reviews.

Wester, W. C. II (1987). *Clinical Hypnosis: A Case Management Approach.* Cincinnati, OH: Behavioral Science Center Inc. Publications.

Wester, W. C. II, & Smith, A. H., Jr. (1991). *Clinical Hypnosis: A Multidisciplinary Approach.* Cincinnati, OH: Behavioral Science Center Inc. Publications.

Williams, K. (2006). Mindfulness-based stress reduction in a worksite wellness program. In R. Baer (Ed.), *Mindfulness-Based Treatment Approaches: Clinician's Guide to Evidence Base and Applications* (pp. 361-375). Burlington, MA: Academic Press.

Williams, M., Teasdale, J., Segal, Z., & Kabat-Zinn, J. (2007). *The Mindful Way Through Depression: Freeing Yourself From Chronic Unhappiness.* New York: Guilford Press.

Wilson, K. G., & DuFrene, T. (2008). *Mindfulness for Two: An Acceptance and Commitment Therapy Approach to Mindfulness in Psychotherapy.* Oakland, CA: New Harbinger.

Wilson, K. G., & DuFrene, T. (2010). *Things Might Go Terribly, Horribly Wrong.* Oakland, CA: New Harbinger.

Wisniewski, L., Safer, D., & Chen, E. (2007). Dialectical behavior therapy and eating disorders. In L. A. Dimeff, K. Koerner, & M. M. Linehan (Eds.), *Dialectical Behavior Therapy in Clinical Practice: Applications Across Disorders and Settings* (pp. 174-221). New York: Guilford Press.

Witkiewitz, K., & Bowen, S. (2010). Depression, craving, and substance use following a randomized trial of mindfulness-based relapse prevention. *Journal of Consulting and Clinical Psychology, 78*(3), 362-374. DOI: 10.1037/a0019172

Witkiewitz, K. A., & Marlatt, G. A. (2007). *Therapist's Guide to Evidence-Based Relapse Prevention.* Boston: Academic Press.

Witkiewitz, K. A., Walker, D., & Marlatt, G. A. (2005). Mindfulness-based relapse prevention for alcohol and substance use disorders. *Journal of Cognitive Psychotherapy: An International Quarterly 19*(3), 211-228.

Wolever, R. Q., & Best, J. L. (2009). Mindfulness-Based approaches to eating disorders. In F. Didonna (Ed.), *Clinical Handbook of Mindfulness* (pp. 259-288). New York: Springer.

Yager, E. (2008). *Foundations of Clinical Hypnosis: From Theory to Practice.* Carmarthen, United Kingdom: Crown House Publishing.

Yalom, I. D. (1980). *Existential Psychotherapy.* New York: Basic Books.

York, M. (2007). A qualitative study into the experience of individuals involved in a mindfulness group within an acute inpatient mental health unit. *Journal of Psychiatric and Mental Health Nursing, 14*(6), 603-608.

Zettle, R. D., & Hayes, S. C. (1987). A component and process analysis of cognitive therapy. *Psychological Reports, 61*, 939-953.

Audio CD of
Mindfulness Practices

On the audio CD that accompanies this book, you will find recordings of specific mindfulness exercises. The recordings are meant to be a quick introduction to mindfulness practices. If they pique your interest, we recommend you find the recordings of Jon Kabat-Zinn, Susan Woods, and others to deepen your practice.

Track 1	Introduction – Richard Sears
Track 2	Body Scan – Richard Sears
Track 3	Sitting Meditation – Richard Sears
Track 4	Three-Minute Breathing Space – Richard Sears
Track 5	Loving-Kindness Meditation – Dennis Tirch
Track 6	Mindfulness for the Clinician – Robert Denton

In making these recordings, the authors would like to acknowledge the influences of and express their appreciation to Stephen K. Hayes, Jon Kabat-Zinn, Zindel Segal, and Susan Woods.

WARNING: These techniques can be very restful and relaxing. DO NOT listen to this CD in the car, when operating dangerous equipment, or when concentration is required.

To Order Additional CDs

Copies of the audio CD in the back of this book may be ordered for colleagues, clients, group members, friends, and others. Although the contents of this CD are copyrighted and may not be copied, you can buy additional legal copies in a hard case. Cost is only $12.95 each plus shipping. If you are ordering 5 or more copies, you will receive a 20% discount.

Your Name _____

Address _____

City _____ State _____ Zip code_____

Telephone: _____ E-mail: _____

Billing (if different than above)

Your Name _____

Address _____

City _____ State _____ Zip code_____

Please send ____ CDs of *Mindfulness Practices* at $12.95 each _____

Shipping/handling:	
1 copy - $5.50	
2 copies - $6.00	
3 copies - $6.50	
4-6 copies - $7.00	
7+ copies - 9% of total	

If ordering 5 or more copies, take 20% discount _____

Subtotal _____

If shipping to a Florida address, add sales tax _____

⟵ Shipping/handling (from table at left) _____

Total _____

Name on credit card:_____

Credit Card #_____ (MasterCard, Visa, Amex)

Exp. date: _____ Security Code (digits on back of MC/Visa or top of Amex) _____

To Order

Go to www.prpress.com • Fax to 866-804-4843 • Call 800-443-3364

Mail to:
Professional Resource Press
PO Box 3197, Sarasota, FL 34230-3197

We reserve the right to correct your calculations if in error.
Prices and shipping charges subject to change without notice.